MW01182043

From the day I first me
journey of 500 intervi
me—was fueled by the dream of answering the question,
it mean to truly live?" In *Bring the Fire*, Holden chases down that
question and reveals the daring adventure of it that we all crave, but
often lose sight of, don't believe is real, or never even knew existed.

—**Mark Batterson,** *New York Times* best selling author of *The
Circle Maker*, lead pastor of National Community Church

Being part of Holden's journey has been a joy. How many sixteen-
year-olds would even start, less finish interviewing 500 Christ-driven
leaders? In *Bring the Fire*, Holden's story will challenge and inspire
you with the truth of what real success is. I urge every young person to
read this book, as it holds value for all of us.

—**David Green,** founder and CEO of Hobby Lobby,
philanthropist

Holden is a determined young man! His compelling desire for answers
led him on a journey of seeking truth from 500 strong Christian
leaders. I am honored to be among the list that he interviewed, and I
trust this book will not only share his inspiring story but also inspire
those who read it.

—**Dr. Joe White,** president and CEO of Kanakuk Ministries

When Holden told me at sixteen that he was going to interview 500
of the top leaders he could find, I didn't expect that he would make it.
Boy, was I wrong. He didn't just cross the finish line of his project, he
blasted over it with blazing passion. But even crazier than Holden's
remarkable project is the story behind it of his desperate search for
truth, life, and God. Buckle up—you're in for an explosive ride.

—**Craig Groeschel,** founder and senior pastor of Life.Church,
New York Times bestselling author

The day I met Holden I saw a mirror image of a younger me: a bit unsure of myself at times, quite overconfident at other times, but desperately wanting to make a difference for Christ. Having watched Holden's journey from a distance, I dare say his story will rekindle a fire for Christ in your life just as it has to mine.

—**David Benham,** serial-entrepreneur,
author of *Whatever the Cost*

When Holden first asked to include me in his project of 500 interviews, I thought here is a young man who might actually be able to accomplish such a gigantic undertaking. And accomplish it he sure did—at a level of great excellence. Bring the Fire pulls together wisdom from hundreds of incredible leaders who have been through life's storms but live all the brighter with God's fire.

—**Cary Summers,** president of Museum of the Bible,
author of *Lifting Up the Bible*

There's little to compare to the gallantry of a young warrior on a righteous quest! Undaunted by the gargantuan task of finding and fulfilling a destiny, Holden fans to flame the embers of our own hearts! It is not "the wisdom of the wise" but the "commonness of the journey" that ignites us in this very raw, but very real transformation! Catch the fire and BRING IT!

—**Dr. Lew Sterrett,** founder of Sermon on the Mount
and Leaders by Heart

Holden lives with a passion that I hope every person gets to experience. A passion comparable to David sprinting to fight Goliath in the Valley of Elah. A passion that will truly change the world if caught. Do me a favor, read this book, catch this fire, and never slow down.

—**Cody Bobay,** founder of Soulcon Ministries

BRING *THE* FIRE

THE GREATEST TRUTHS

I LEARNED IN HIGH SCHOOL

BY INTERVIEWING 500

CHRIST-DRIVEN LEADERS

HOLDEN HILL

CEDAR GATE PUBLISHING

ISBN 978-0-9997117-0-5

Editor: Dudley Delffs
Cover design: Saturday's Gravy, Heston Hill Photography, Holden Hill

Printed in the United States of America

To the Warriors:
Alone, one might make a difference.
Together, we can change the world.
Come on, let's go change the world together!

CONTENTS

CRAIG GROESCHEL

When Holden Hill told me he was going to interview 500 of the greatest leaders he could find, I remember thinking, "That's an amazing goal, but I bet he doesn't get past fifty before he wears out and quits."

I'm so glad I didn't bet against this visionary young leader.

As Holden's pastor and a family friend, I've had the privilege of knowing him since he was a child. I've seen Holden crash four-wheelers, jump off buildings, send himself flying down snow-covered slopes, and survive one daredevil feat after another. At the same time, I've seen him move audiences with passionate speeches, mentor countless other young men, and grow as a leader, worshiper, and follower of Christ.

Holden is both an ordinary kid and, simultaneously, an extraordinary visionary. As someone once said, "The difference between ordinary and extraordinary is a little bit extra." And that's what Holden exemplifies—a little bit extra.

As you read his book, I think you will agree. Let's be honest: What does it take for an unknown, homeschooled teenager from Oklahoma to get face-to-face time with Dave Ramsey, Christine Caine, Sadie Robertson, Mark Batterson, Lecrae, and 495 other world-class leaders? The answer is "a little bit extra."

A little extra vision.

A little extra passion.

A little extra persistence.

A little extra effort.

And a little extra courage.

When I asked Holden about his biggest takeaway from completing 500 interviews, he replied without hesitation, "A life worth living isn't about getting all you can get. It's about giving it everything you've got. Hands down. Life is a journey, and if you're only trying to get something for yourself, you will never go far. We only go our furthest and live to our fullest when it's for others."

So get ready to be inspired, equipped, and empowered. This book, and Holden's example, will move you to invest in others instead of living for yourself. It will move you to want to make others see God through you, instead of wanting to be seen. It will inspire you to live by faith instead of fearing failure. And instead of playing it safe, you will find courage to take risks.

You may be tempted to dive into this book as you would any other one. But let me suggest that you read it S-L-O-W-L-Y.

Keep a pen in hand.

Underline and take notes.

Write your questions.

Record your takeaways and goals.

Read again and repeat!

As you engage with Holden and his journey, I believe a contagious spark of passion will start to burn in your soul. As Ferdinand Foch said, "The most powerful force on earth is the human soul on fire."

So open up your heart.

Get ready to learn.

Get ready to grow.

Get ready to give.

Get ready to catch fire, live it, and bring it.

And be amazed at all God will do!

SPARK OF LIFE

"What does it mean to really, truly live?"

The question rumbled through my consciousness like a dance-music bass drop. I was ten years old and had just finished watching the movie *Braveheart* with my dad and two younger brothers for the first time. Falling asleep in the camping trailer where we were staying that night, I couldn't shake the memory of a line said by William Wallace in the movie: "Every man dies, not every man really lives."

Normally, ten-year-old boys tend to dismiss deep, profound dialogue as nothing more than an annoying pause in the action, but not this time. This time, the words touched my curiosity like tongues of fire, intensifying the spark of wonder that already burned inside me.

Ever since I was old enough to think about and process the world around me, I've noticed a difference that exists between two different kinds of people: those who live with a burning passion, raging love, and sense of adventure roaring inside them, and those who don't. Early on as a child, I hadn't been able to articulate that difference—I had just known subtly, in the back of my mind, that somehow, breathing and living weren't always the same thing.

But now, after hearing *Braveheart* put words to the very mystery I'd wondered about for so long, I knew one thing: whatever it meant to really, truly live, I wanted it. Even if, at the time, I had no idea what that meant.

While technically I grew up being homeschooled, my childhood would probably be better described as "road-schooled." My dad is an entrepreneur, and I was constantly on the move with him—either in black Calvin Klein dress shoes, traveling the country and shaking hands with business executives, or in camouflage Under Armour work boots at our 320-acre property, operating bulldozers alongside construction contractors.

As a young boy, I knew right off the bat that life felt awfully boring without fun in it, and it didn't take me much longer to learn that it also felt terribly empty without work in it. So, as I grew older, I decided to go full throttle when it came to both fun and work.

No matter what it was—be it working at our land, developing a project of mine, or fighting through basketball practice—I would push myself like an animal. And whenever it came to fun, I pushed myself even harder. I took bigger risks and hustled harder each time I tried something new. In the end, my philosophy was pretty simple: Why ever go halfway in life when the goal is to live to the fullest?

By the time I hit high school, I thought I was starting to figure out the answer to my childhood question. As far as I could tell, everyone was initially born with the spark of life—wonder, passion, and thirst for adventure—but somewhere along the journey of life, most people sold their spark in exchange for safety, ease, and comfort.

As for me, I refused to ever sell out. I thought Jesus had gotten it pretty spot-on when he asked the question, "What does it profit a man to gain the whole world and lose his soul?" And so that's why, during my high school years, my answer to the question "What does it mean to truly live?" eventually became what I called "living on fire."

I thought that the answer to "truly living" was to breathe life into your passions. It was to chisel yourself into the absolute best you could be. It was to live a life so fearless and free that everyone on the planet would say, "I just wish I could live a life as amazing as yours." I thought that like a bonfire, the more fuel you fed into your life, the warmer and brighter it would become, and the less fuel you fed into it, the colder and emptier it would become. And so, for a long time, I committed myself to filling my life with what I considered "fuel"—popularity, image, and adrenaline-junkie-adventure.

But it only worked to a certain point.

When I was sixteen years old I thought I knew what truly living was supposed to be, but for some reason, my source of "fuel" no longer worked. My popularity wasn't enough. My image was becoming boring. And all the adrenaline in the world couldn't replace my deep longing for something more—though I didn't know what. So, in 2014, I set out on a mission to meet and interview 500 passionate, courageous, pioneering Christian leaders with the goal of learning about life and, hopefully, what it was that I was missing.

Throughout my project, I probably asked a hundred-thousand different questions, but all of those questions were born out of four bedrock layer questions manifested by my depiction of what truly living meant. It's those questions that make the structure of this book:

What does it take to live with passion?

Who am I, really?

How do I become fearless?

Why is this all worth it?

In the beginning of my project, I had life all figured out—or at least, I told myself I did. Truly living meant taking every ounce of passion, energy, determination, and fight that I possessed and using it to make my life as full as possible. Because, after all, the more I could get out of life the fuller I could make my own, right?

And so, I refused to just exist—baby, I wanted to *live on fire!* Because from my viewpoint, that's what it meant to truly live in the way I'd heard the movie *Braveheart* and others describe. And, to a degree, "living on fire" is what it means to truly live.

But that's not all it means. No, not even close.

The truth is far more dangerous, far more difficult, and infinitely better than I had ever dared to imagine.

DISCLAIMER

My journey to interview 500 Christ-driven leaders began over three years ago, and if I had written this book back then, when I had just started, you would be reading a completely different story right now. This book would be nothing more than a self-enamored chronicle of my greatest successes in life, written only in the hope that people would be impressed with me.

Have you ever been a cocky, insecure, arrogant snot who thought they knew everything? I have. That's exactly who I was three years ago.

Some would say that I still am an arrogant snot, and to an extent, maybe they're right. But it might be more accurate to say that without Christ, I'm a weak, broken person who learned as a boy to hide his insecurities behind a mask of strobe-light arrogance and attitude, and who still struggles with doing so.

Throughout the years of grinding through my interview project, however, I was resoundingly humbled unlike anything I'd ever experienced before. Have you ever had your ego picked up, slammed against the ground, and shattered into a thousand pieces? I have.

So here's the disclaimer: this book wasn't written by someone who's perfect, who has all the answers figured out, or who has everything nailed down. For the most part, I've grown up in Oklahoma under the guidance and protection of my awesome parents. I'm young and just barely out of high school, and heck, I've never even had a real full-time job.

I'm not writing this book because I think I know a bunch of stuff you don't, but to inspire you with what God has shown me through my own journey of seeking wisdom from 500 faith-filled, Christ-driven leaders. This book was written by an ordinary teenager who is on a journey of growth and discovery just as much as you are.

Chapter 1

INSANITY

"Everyone has gifts and talents, and if you find those they'll take you places. But to find your purpose, you first have to find God."

—Lecrae Moore,

rapper, hip-hop recording artist, interview #8

"I'm going insane..."

The thought had saturated my mind for weeks, bleeding through the very fabric of my sanity. I felt, for lack of a better word, *fake*—so fake, in fact, that I started habitually looking in the mirror just to make sure it was still me looking back at myself. But the person in the mirror didn't look like me, either. I felt like I was a passenger trapped inside someone else's mind, slowly suffocating to death and unable to escape to the open air.

The previous month, my basketball team had finished our season as the 2014 homeschool junior varsity national champions, the school year had ended, and I'd turned sixteen. For most people, I guess a trifecta like this would be a really sweet and satisfying point in life, but not for me.

Recently, I'd been growing increasingly agitated with life and my attitude toward it. A part of me deep down demanded I stop trying to fit in with everyone else, that I stand and fight for what I believed in, and that I live the adventure I so desperately longed for—whatever that was. I longed to change, but I couldn't. Wouldn't. But I had to, because if something didn't change, I felt like I would die.

When I had started playing basketball four years earlier, I'd loved it. I hadn't been a very skilled player back then, but had been strong and fast enough to make up for it. From my first game on, I had been a starting player and team leader.

Then, just a year ago when I had switched teams to play with a higher-level organization, my high-rolling ego had plummeted.

Things were good at first, but once the season commenced and we started having games, I found myself playing a position I'd never played before: benchwarmer. I was often lucky to even make it on the court, and that didn't sit well with me. But, what could I do about it?

At first, I decided just to keep my head down and grind. I pushed myself like an animal in practice, I worked on shots and handles all day on my driveway, and I never let myself be out-hustled. But no matter what I did, I was simply less skilled than the majority of my team—and since our goal was to actually outscore the opposing team and not just out-hustle them, I continued to get minuscule playing time.

I ranked among the lowest on the roster. No one looked up to me. My words of encouragement to people were white noise. I didn't dare challenge someone to push themselves harder when I was the very one responsible for losing a ball and making us lose our last game. I was no one. And so, that's when I unintentionally reverted to a ploy, designed by fear, that I've battled ever since: fitting in.

Forget encouraging and challenging people to be better. No one cared what I had to say, anyway. I started paying attention to the kinds of jokes the starters made, the way they talked, and the way they acted, and I began replicating them. I talked about my friends behind their backs just to fit in with people. I said things I hated myself for, just to fit in. I refrained from standing up for people because I knew if I dared stand up for them, I would compromise my ability to fit in. Whatever it was, I did what I had to do to fit in.

It worked, and it didn't. It worked because I actually did manage to start fitting in, but it didn't work because fitting in only made me feel worse. Eventually, I reached a point where I was trying so hard to fit in—not just with my basketball team, but also with people in general—that my personality, style, and character were almost beyond recognition. I had mutilated and contorted myself into something I thought other people might like, or if not like then at least notice. And I hated myself for it.

That's why I had decided to quit basketball after the season was over. Forget my fear of once again being an outcast—if I ran this mindless lap of fitting in one more time, I was going to explode. It was almost as if, at that point in my life, even my fear of rejection was finally overshadowed by something else: my fear of arriving at death without ever truly living in the first place.

Once I made up my mind that I was done playing basketball, I immediately started brainstorming with my dad on what I should focus the next season of my life toward. Making money was an obvious factor to consider since I was now old enough to drive and wanted a vehicle, but though I kept quiet about it, I considered another factor even more important: whatever the next phase of my life was, it had to be crazy, because crazy was the only way I knew of to keep myself from going insane. And after brainstorming on and off with my dad for a few weeks, an idea wild enough was born.

Dad had recently interviewed several young college graduates who had been job searching for several months and now hoped to find a position in our company, but none of them had really fit the bill. However, my dad, my brother, and I had been reading through the Book of Proverbs recently, and my dad had been captivated by its counsel that wisdom is "gained through the counsel of many" (Prov. 15:22).

So, when my dad ended up having to turn the college graduates away, he did so with some advice. Since they'd been unsuccessful in securing a job so far, what if they go ask for meetings with some of the most successful business owners in Oklahoma—say, 100 of them—and seek to learn what those people were looking for in young hires?

At that point in time, I was interested in working with the sales team of our company to learn skills like connecting with people, building trust and relationships with customers, networking, cold calling, etc. And I also wanted to start making money.

However, my plans were about to change. None of the recent college graduates ended up pursuing my dad's idea, but that didn't mean Dad stopped thinking about it. Before long, he decided to share the idea with me.

The day Dad dragged me into his home office and told me the idea, I fell in love with it immediately. It was wildly crazy, original, unpredictable, and everything else I'd always thought "truly living" was meant to be. However, there were two initial changes I needed to make: first, I didn't want to talk only with business owners. I wanted to learn from leaders, risk takers, visionaries, entrepreneurs, pastors, innovators, performers, athletes, and warriors of God's kingdom— people from all across life's spectrum.

And secondly, talking with 100 people seemed too basic for my ambitious sixteen-year-old self. I asked my dad to estimate how many sales calls he might have made the first year of starting our family company, and he guessed around 500. With that number, I knew the end goal of my project: interview 500 leaders.

As much as I loved the idea in the beginning, I still had one problem with it: I wanted money to buy a vehicle, and to the best of my knowledge, interviewing successful gurus wasn't directly profitable. However, by this time my dad had come to believe so strongly in this potential project and the impact it could have on me that he proposed a winning solution: after the 500 interviews were complete, he would buy a vehicle for me.

Despite the fabrications I starting making up to tell other people about my desire to "learn and grow as a person," my motivation for the interview project was far more specific. As far as I was concerned, I had just come out of the most suffocating time in my life, and I never wanted to go back. I hated bowing to the opinions of others. I hated being white noise. And I hated following the crowd. Desperate to get as far away as possible from the fear I'd been living in, I vowed to never again live to fit in.

But little did I know that, by using that same desperation, fear was already sowing its next ambition into my mind: make people impressed with me, instead.

Ground Zero

It didn't take long for me to turn my world inside out. Leveraging my social circles, social media, innate capacity for risk and adventure, and new project of interviews, I devoted myself more than ever to building what I considered "the perfect persona." Everything I did screamed, "I'm bold, confident, and fearless. My life is awesome. I'm going to travel the country and interview incredible people. I'm amazing, don't you think?" I don't know how many other people bought the lies I started covering myself in, but I know I sure did.

Before long, I managed to put all my distasteful past out of memory and convince myself that I was actually this new, flashy, cocky hotshot. But then came an opportunity that, as far as I was concerned, shot a hole in my perfect persona. That opportunity was a chance to talk with Dr. Ben Carson.

Dr. Ben Carson, the bestselling author and retired surgeon who had been Director of Pediatric Neurosurgery at Johns Hopkins University, was on a book-signing tour and was having a signing event just a few miles from my house. My mom was, and still is a huge fan of Dr. Carson, and several months prior to his upcoming visit, she had forced me and all my siblings to read his autobiographical book, *Gifted Hands*. The book captures the story of how he grew up in poverty in Detroit and ended up becoming a brilliant neurosurgeon who pioneered many different operations, including the only successful separation of conjoined twins.

Dr. Carson would go on to run for president as a Republican candidate in 2016, but as my family and I were standing in line to meet him at his book signing, all I could think about was the immediate opportunity opening before me. *"Why not talk with him and make him the first person in my interview journey?"* I thought. But I had plenty of reasons as to why not.

For one, I would only have enough time to ask one question. There would be no drawn out, full conversation with Dr. Carson. I thought back to real, professional interviews I'd seen on news and media outlets performed between famous news anchors or TV hosts and their important, high-caliber guests. *"Isn't that how interviews are supposed to be?"* I thought to myself. My "question" was a joke compared to what I thought an actual interview was supposed to look like.

To take away from the glamour and glitter of the situation even more, I was going to be meeting Dr. Carson at a book signing. Egocentric anger boiled inside me as I thought, *"A book signing?! That's how this all begins? Anyone could talk with Dr. Carson in a book signing—I refuse to be so generic!"*

However, after waging civil war in my mind for a few minutes, torn between foregoing this opportunity or seizing it despite the unromantic beginning I thought it would give my journey, I eventually realized something: this first opportunity wasn't what would make or break the significance of my project—that would be determined by what I made of this opportunity.

And really, this was an awesome opportunity, even though it might not seem perfect. But if I decided to forgo this chance, I may never see it—or Dr. Carson—again.

At that point, I made up my mind. In a book signing line with a single question, I was going to make Dr. Ben Carson the starting interview. It was time for ground zero.

When the line finally brought me forward for my turn to shake Dr. Carson's hand, I said, "Hello, Dr. Carson, my name's Holden! I had a quick question: What's your most important word of advice to the next generation of our country?"

He looked at me with deep, wise eyes, and after thinking about it for a second, responded, "Get a grasp on fiscal responsibility." I smiled big and thanked him for his answer, then got my book signed and my picture taken with him.

And that's how it started. With just one question.

Hundreds of people had the same opportunity I did that day to talk with Dr. Carson, but I'll bet few others were as radically impacted by it as I was. Why? It wasn't because of the opportunity itself—everyone had the same opportunity I did. It was because of what I would come to make of that opportunity.

That was the first step of my incredible, crazy journey of the next three years. I didn't know what it would look like in the end, but I took the opportunity to talk with Dr. Carson, regardless, and began to build it into what I wanted it to be. As Eric Newman, screenwriter and author of several films including *Home Run*, later told me in our interview, "The more you develop something, the more it tells you what it needs to be."

That day, I learned an opportunity is simply a chance to begin. What becomes of that opportunity—well, that's up to you.

More Than Coincidence

For the next couple of weeks, I focused on writing down questions I wanted to ask, brainstorming on topics I wanted to cover, and making a "hit list" of people I wanted to seek out and make part of my project. And I conducted more interviews.

The next three people I interviewed were friends of my dad, men I knew and respected who would soon become mentors of mine throughout my project. Joe Williams, the President of Oklahoma National Christian Foundation, followed by Boe Parrish, a pastor and the founder and CEO of Corporate Care, and then Lew Sterrett, a wild stallion horse trainer and leadership speaker.

As I became more comfortable asking questions and holding intentional conversations with my interviewees, I learned to relax a little and enjoy the process. Some of the ideas and perspectives people had on life were actually quite interesting. In fact, something I picked up on right away was that all three of the people I interviewed after Dr. Carson had a very similar outlook on life as I did, except with one major difference: I wanted to make the most of life for myself, while these people wanted to make the most of life for *God*.

That idea was confusing to me. Sure, I believed God existed, but why would I live for him? The two of us already had a deal: I obeyed his rules, and he would get me to heaven. As a bonus, we even talked and hung out sometimes. Wasn't that enough?

I thought so. I kept God on the back-burner to make sure I had someone to go to for support in case I ever felt sad, scared, or hurt. He was real to me when I needed him, but whenever I didn't, he got pushed to the side as I resumed my place at the center of the universe.

However, the following month I had the chance to interview someone in a radical, totally unpredictable way, and it changed everything.

Here's what went down. Toward the end of summer, some friends and I were volunteering at Kanakuk Kamps in Branson, Missouri, at their family camp: K-Kauai. It was the end of our first week volunteering. The campers from the previous week had left that morning, and the campers for the next week were coming in that evening.

In between, the rest of the volunteer force and I had a few hours of downtime to relax, and that's when I first heard the rumor that Lecrae and his family would be among the group of new campers coming in. Lecrae, as you may know, is an amazing performer and songwriter: a Christian hip hop artist and rapper known for his raw honesty about life and about God's grace.

By that evening, other counselors had confirmed that Lecrae would indeed be there but they also warned us not to bother him while he was "on vacation." Nevertheless, you can imagine what popped into my mind when I realized my proximity to such an incredible, inspiring young Christian artist. Immediately, I started thinking of how I could meet him. I was hungry for people's infatuation, and as far as I was concerned, making Lecrae part of my project was a sure way to get it.

It had been over a month since I'd started my project and I had now interviewed six more people since Dr. Ben Carson. Most were influential leaders in Oklahoma who were friends of my dad. I found the gig fun and interesting, but not that important. It was still just my way of building an image for myself and earning a car. However, all that was about to change.

What's crazy is that I was actually supposed to have gone home from camp the previous week. On the first day we had all arrived, I had found out some of my friends were staying an extra week, so after getting my parents' permission—which had come much easier than I'd expected—I'd asked the camp coordinators if I could extend my stay.

While technically I was supposed to have set that up with the coordinators the week earlier, by some stroke of "luck" it worked out for me to stay the extra week—which turned out to be the same week Lecrae was there. I don't typically believe in coincidence, and this is no exception. Throughout my life, I've learned that sometimes it's the places you don't think you're supposed to be that land you right where God wants you.

Hip-Hop Hope

"You got this. You know how to get people to like you. Everyone will think you're amazing. Why are you shaking? Come on, focus."

Thoughts exploded through my head as I tried to keep cool. It was off-time on the second day of camp and I was walking to the pool in a tank top and pair of boardshorts. Up ahead, Lecrae and his son were walking toward me on the same sidewalk, likely on their way to "The

Bean", the camp drink and snack shop I had just come from that was adjoined to the dinning hall.

"Fifteen paces. Ten paces. Five paces." I counted down the distance in my head. Then, before I knew it, we were maneuvering to our own sides of the sidewalk to pass each other.

"Say something," I told myself. But I couldn't. So I screamed into my mind, commanding my mouth to speak. But no matter my surging need for people's acceptance and infatuation, it wasn't enough to overcome the fear suffocating me. Fear of what? I didn't even know. I was just scared. And without the strength to act in the face of it, I walked right past Lecrae with nothing more than a nod and a smile.

When I arrived at the pool moments later I buried my face in my right-hand palm and closed my eyes, absolutely devastated. Sure, missing the opportunity to talk with Lecrae was frustrating, but that was small compared to what was really bothering me.

"What am I even doing?" I thought. Here I was serving at one of my favorite summer camps, getting to hang with some of my best friends, and bordering on the chance of meeting Lecrae—yet I was living out of fear as much as I ever had, scrambling for people's acceptance of me.

With a deep breath I calmed my mind, and then as I pulled my hand down across my face and reopened my eyes, I prayed a prayer I'll never forget. Beneath my breath, I asked God, *"Father, give me a second chance"*—and he did.

As the week rolled by, my hopes sank further and further. Because of my schedule in the kitchen I only had a couple hours of free time each day, and so far, Lecrae and I hadn't crossed paths again since that first time on the sidewalk. Before I knew it, it was the last day of camp and I was still out of luck.

By cleanup time after dinner, I had almost completely resigned myself to reality. Everyone was leaving camp the next morning. I'd blown my one shot, and that was it. But then, in the span of a few seconds, my whole world changed. As I was helping stack chairs and clean tables, I saw Lecrae enter the snack and drink shop I had suspected he was headed to the first time I saw him—the one adjoined to the dinning hall. I knew in an instant that this was the second chance I'd asked God for. There likely wouldn't be another.

At that moment, fear gripped me like a vice as it had many times before, pouring its venom into me and whispering in my ear. I was paralyzed. Not because the situation scared me but because the mere idea of standing up to fear after cowering to it for so long was terrifying. I'd spent the past year drifting with the current; what made me think I had what it took to suddenly disturb it? But at the same time, that might have been the greatest motivation I could have.

After conforming to fear's commands for so long, the prospect of breaking fear was suddenly irresistible. Not in the cool, daredevil way I was used to, and not for the purpose of getting people to be impressed with me as was usually the case. No, that's how I'd gone about trying to meet him previously, but not this time. This time, my resolve wasn't built around being a hotshot, it was built around being truly brave in the pursuit of an opportunity I knew God was giving me. I couldn't chicken out this time—if I did, I felt I might die.

Since the last time I'd tried to talk with Lecrae, I'd learned my lesson: if you give fear enough time to talk you out of something, it will. So, in order to beat fear to the punch, I took immediate action. Without a single question ready or any plan of how I was going to do it, I finished flipping a chair on top of a table, marched to the coffee house, and walked up to Lecrae. I introduced myself and asked with genuine curiosity the first question that came to my mind: "What's your most important word of wisdom to the next generation of Christian leaders?"

My question was extremely abrupt, but it worked. Lecrae put down his ice cream cone and we started talking. A minute later my friend Ethan walked up beside me, squatted down as I was, and said he would like to listen in on our conversation. As Lecrae and I talked more, I made a mental note to remember, if nothing else, his answer to my first question.

He'd said, "Man, one thing to your generation… I'd tell you that everyone has gifts and talents, and if you find those they'll take you places. But to find your purpose, you first have to find God."

When I went to bed that night, the storm of thoughts swirling in my mind wouldn't let me fall asleep, and they all circled one relentless question: Why had Lecrae talked with me?

Well, duh, because I'd marched up to him and asked him a question. But why had he taken an interest in me, answered my questions with thought and intention, and allowed me to continue our conversation well past the point he could have reasonably excused himself? He got *nothing* from me. I wasn't famous, I wasn't rich, I wasn't even one of the camp counselors. I was only a sixteen-year-old kid who was volunteering in the kitchen, yet Lecrae had taken the time to talk with me. So, why?

Laying in my bunk-bed, thoughts continued rushing through my mind like water, steadily uncovering and bringing to the surface all the deep-set wonder that had been buried for so long. For the first time in a long while, fear wasn't there to suppress it. And out of all those stirred up thoughts and ideas, the one that demanded my attention the most was my childhood question, "What does it mean and what does it take to really, truly live?" Despite the flashy, impressive life I tried to live, the real truth behind that question remained a mystery to me.

It was then that I conceived an idea, an idea that carried more power and raw life than I'd felt since the beginning of my project: What if this project could be about so much more than my ego and getting a car? Surely, God had given me the second chance at talking with Lecrae for so much more than to look cool in front of my friends. I trembled as I considered the possibility. What if God was giving me this project as a way for me to find the truth behind the question I'd asked for so long?

In a split second, the idea took root deep inside me. I suddenly felt incredibly alive, like I had just discovered something worth living for.

I didn't know then what I would eventually build my project into over the next year and a half, or that after the interview phase I would end up spending another year and a half writing a book on it. But in that moment, what I did know was that whatever I did build my project into, I was going to find my answer through it. I had to.

Since that day, I've come to learn that meaning and purpose in life are usually fueled by obsession, not reason. Of course, misplaced obsession can easily destroy a person. But as I laid in my camp bunk-bed staring at the ceiling, my mind vibrant with imagination and dreams, the obsession gently coming to life inside me was simple: discover the truth.

The next week, after I got home from Kanakuk, my new sense of purpose and passion set me into whirling motion. I went crazy asking my parents and other family friends for contacts of leaders they knew and respected—people who were influential, visionary, driven, adventurous, brave, passionate, wise, impactful, and making a difference for Christ. And whenever I found someone I thought might be worth reaching out to, I'd call or email them.

I had plenty of emails and voicemails that were never responded to, and I had people decline my request for a meeting. I even had a few people hang up on me because of my sometimes nervous and stammering voice, but I hardly noticed those times. I was too focused on the adventure.

I didn't realize it at first, but that day I had prayed for a second chance at talking with Lecrae, God also answered it with a second chance at something else: chasing the journey of 500 interviews not as a way of getting approval and a vehicle, but as a search for truth and, ultimately, Him.

What For?

What are you living for? Do you know? Or do you even want to know? After all, it's more comfortable to live lukewarm than for your purpose, isn't it? It's like we enjoy God so long as he's just there to warm our emotions like a heater in our basement, but nothing more, because then we'd have to surrender control.

But then again, if we can't lose ourselves to what's worth living for, what's the point of living at all?

One person I met in the beginning of my journey and who would end up becoming a big part of it was Joe White, the CEO of Kanakuk Kamps. Still running off the high of my new project vision, I remember once asking Joe a question I'd been asking myself recently: "Why is it that so many people seem to go through life feeling empty and devoid of passion and purpose? Like they've forgotten what they're living for?"

His answer had been, "I see lives changed and hearts set on fire when people become bondservants to Christ. When they walk daily in step with the Holy Spirit. Because when you identify with the purpose God has planted in your heart and really begin to know him, life is far from bland or purposeless."

At the time, Joe's answer to me sounded typical. I'd heard it before: the secret to a fulfilling, passionate, and meaningful life was Jesus.

"Yeah, sure. Then why is there so much evidence to the contrary? Like, the vast number of Christians who still seem to do nothing more than just exist?" I thought.

However, there was something more to Joe's answer that took me time to notice and understand. Joe didn't tell me that the source of a passionate life was Jesus, but rather, walking *with* him every day.

Another person I posed the question to in the following weeks was Tim Ulrich, a former Californian who took a downtown Oklahoma City hub for drug addicts and prostitutes and turned it into a ministry community for the homeless. Tim's answer was, "Christians try to escape from the culture instead of engaging it. That's why Christians can often be found without meaning or purpose."

I remember when Tim told me that, something clicked for me. Suddenly, I found myself seeing what he, Joe White, and others had been talking to me about, and I was completely taken by it!

Often in life, it's easy for us to fall into playing defense. Protecting what we have and what we've achieved, we manage to stay where we are. But that's not what we were born for. And the more we live in defense, the more we die each day—not for lack of food and water, but for lack of faith in God. After all, man does not live by bread alone, and what kind of faith is it that we stop chasing God to instead protect the security we find in the world?

As believers, I find that many of us lose our passion not because we stop believing God is real, but because we stop caring. We're no longer desperately in love with him. We're no longer obsessed. As a result, we're left with a heart that longs for Christ's battle-cry of hope, but that we neglect to instead protect our little bubble of comfort and security. In the end, we miss the point. As my friend Kent Bresee, an entrepreneur, once told me, "If you only live preventing what you don't want to happen, you will end up sabotaging what you want the most."

So let me ask again: what are you living for? And this time, let's take it a step further: do your actions say the same thing? Because if all you ever do is prevent what you don't want to happen, then I know from personal experience that the main thing you're living for is likely fear. To find true life, stop living in reactionary defense. You'll only succeed in making yourself tired. Instead, go on the offense against hell and start bringing heaven to earth.

In those early days of my project, though I wasn't fully aware, I was starting to learn something then that would come to shape the rest of my life. Now realizing what it felt like to be obsessed with finding the truth behind my own question, I was simultaneously learning a part of what walking with Jesus should feel like: All in. Sold out. Passionate. Desperate. Perhaps what even some would call insane.

Because after all, everyone is born with the spark of life inside them, but only those crazy enough to commit all the way ever truly catch fire.

Chapter 2

DARE TO DREAM

"Anyone can change from passive to passionate at any time,
they just have to decide why they're doing it. If you get a big
enough 'why,' you'll get in gear."

—Dave Ramsey,
motivational speaker, author, radio host, interview #250

"Heston, attach the GoPro to the dashboard!" I suddenly exclaimed as I turned off the music blasting through our vehicle's speakers.

Heston, my younger brother, immediately caught hold of my urgency, rummaged through his bag for his GoPro—the action video camera—and hurriedly locked it into place on the GoPro mount we had attached to the pickup dashboard. He hit the record button and we started making commentary.

"What's up everyone! Heston, tell 'em where we're headed!" I announced.

"Hey guys! So Holden and I are cutting across Edmond right now toward Kilpatrick Turnpike. My family's meeting us at a car shop where we're going to drop off the pickup, and then we're all going on to Crested Butte, Colorado from there!"

I jumped in again. "Yeah! We try to go every year as a family to hit the slopes! Heston skis, I snowboard, and this trip we wanted to make a video to capture the entire trip."

The commentary continued as we talked about things we wanted to do and memories from years past.

This was far from our first time to film a video. The most recent video we'd done was a longboarding video around the perimeter of our local lake, and prior to that, Heston and I had been making short adventure-style videos for years. However, this would be the most extensive, high-caliber video we'd ever done to date. And honestly, we were more excited now than we'd ever been for any project in the past.

The next day, we spent the entire road trip filming each other and telling stories to the camera. We rolled down the windows to film the giant mountains enclosing us on either side as we cut across country, and we used a suction-cup mount to attach the GoPro to the roof of our Suburban and create time-lapse videos as cars streamed past us and the road blurred beneath.

When we finally arrived in Crested Butte, I reached beneath the car seat and grabbed my homemade GoPro stick—a four-foot-long branch of pinewood that I'd dried out, whittled on, and attached a mount to. I attached my GoPro to the end of it and started swinging it around as I filmed the excited reactions of my family pouring into our rental cabin.

After we'd brought all of the stuff inside, I took my snowboard, boots, and luggage back to my bedroom, where I threw it all in a big heap and changed into my snow boots.

The next day, we hit the slopes. GoPros filming away, we took the Silver Queen lift up the mountain as a family and enjoyed the morning together. Heston and I would sometimes switch places to film each other—making jumps, attempting tricks, spraying snow, sliding on rails, and wiping out. We filmed ourselves drinking hot chocolate, our feet kicked up against the fire pit, and talking about the runs of the day. One morning, Heston and my dad got up extra early to capture the sunrise with my family's DJI drone that we'd recently bought. We filmed everything.

On the last run of the trip, I decided to try a jump I'd been eying all week. It was bigger than any I'd tried before, and I had been scared until now to try it, but this was the last day. If I got hurt now, we were going home anyway. I told Heston my intention, and he went ahead of me and stopped at the peak of the ramp—GoPro in hand and ready to film.

I took a deep breath and then launched myself down the slope. As soon as I hit the ramp and felt myself leave the ground, I tucked my knees up into my chest, grabbed the edge of my board, and let myself enjoy the feeling of soaring through the air for a moment. Then I extended my legs back out with a slight bend still in my knees to absorb the impact of landing. I'd nailed it.

Later that night, we fulfilled an annual tradition of ours by digging out a snow cave in the six-foot-deep snow behind our cabin and building a campfire in the center of it. We all brought pieces of wood from the garage or pizza boxes from the house to sit on and enjoyed the warm heat of the fire as we talked, listened to Dad play the guitar, and looked at the stars.

Heston and I buzzed around, getting video footage of our family and the blazing fire from different angles. Heston even conducted a brief interviewing session where he filmed our family members and questioned them on what their favorite part of the week had been.

In all, we killed it that trip. Most people who see our short video will think we simply went to Colorado with our GoPros, did some cool stunts, and shot it in the course of a week. But truth be told, it wasn't in one week—Heston and I had been building up to this point since we were boys.

Take Your Shot

Heston and I have actively worked together and alongside friends of ours to capture and create adventure-style films since we were nine and eleven years old, respectively—before either of us even had our first crush on a girl. And it's through our journey of filmmaking together that I've learned to go big, you have to start small.

When we went to Colorado, we didn't have a multimillion-dollar blockbuster budget to make a film on. We just had a couple of GoPros, a cool road trip, and a DJI drone. But there was a time when even to have all that would have been mind-blowing to us.

In the very beginning, when we were just starting out, the extent of our filming equipment had been nothing more than the webcam of an old MacBook I owned. Heston, me, and our friend Brendan had literally started making films by acting out our different roles, while I or someone else would film the scene by holding my MacBook at an angle so that the keyboard didn't get in the shot.

Then, one day, my dad said we could use his iPhone 3GS for videos. That day, he might as well have given us a full-fledged production camera!

It seems like a lot of people secretly have daring dreams and audacious ideas, but most of them never do anything to pursue those dreams because the odds against them seem so unbeatable. But the fact is, to chase a great dream, you will always have to face great odds. For Heston, me, and our film gang, we were cursed with feelings of futility.

All we had at first was that MacBook webcam for a camera. We weren't even teenagers yet. We didn't have any money. We weren't famous. We didn't live in Hollywood. The extent of our cast and crew was our circle of friends. The only outlet we had to share our work was YouTube. But we refused to let any of that stop us, and chose instead to see the challenges we faced as an opportunity to be creative.

Since those beginnings, Heston and I have failed in film over and over again. I've tried to start up three different YouTube channels alongside my friends, and each one of them has failed. Heston started off creating short video clips to post on Instagram that, looking back on now, he finds embarrassing to watch. Heston and I have filmed countless videos of each other, from relaxing around a fire to driving four-wheelers at full throttle, and many of them have ended up serving no greater purpose than taking up storage in a forgotten archive file. Yet we've refused to give up.

One thing I've learned in life is that it will always be easier to come up with excuses to quit than it will be to come up with reasons to persevere. But what I've also learned is that while the easy path is comfortable, it's also empty, because it's the level of odds you conquer in achieving your dream that determines if the journey is an adventure, if crossing the finish line is sweet, and if the story is worth retelling.

If you'll dare to move in faith by starting where you are with what you have, and if you'll refuse to give up, the challenges and odds you face will make a champion out of you. How? Because sometimes, God uses his most trusted and well-trained warriors to fight the most daunting and important battles, but I find that just as often, He uses the most daunting and important battles to forge his most trusted and well-trained warriors. As Jon Gordon, a leadership speaker and author, told me during our interview, "God doesn't choose the best, he chooses the most willing."

If you know the story of David and Goliath, you also know David could have made every excuse known to man. Just for starters, he was a teenage shepherd boy who was too inexperienced with warfare to even wear body armor properly, let alone adequately wield a sword. His challenger came in the form of a ten-foot-tall warlord named Goliath. The king himself, who was one of the most seasoned and battle-hewn warriors in all of Israel, urged David to forgo facing Goliath. Those reasons alone are stronger grounds for giving up than I've ever had. But David would have none of it.

David abandoned the ranks of the Israelite army and began making his way toward the giant who stood in front of the Philistine battle line. Before long, he was close enough for Goliath to size him up and see he was no more than a boy. Goliath, disgusted with the fact that a little boy was wasting his time, scorned and mocked him.

Still, David wasn't swayed. David yelled a death sentence at the Philistine and then, with a sling in his hand and no more than shepherd's clothing on his back, charged the giant. As the two thundered closer, David slung a stone from his sling and sunk it square into Goliath's forehead, killing him instantly. And then, with Goliath's own sword, David beheaded him.

Excuses don't win battles, they don't burn calories, and they don't build warriors. Playing basketball, I took to heart my coach's point that you will miss 100% of all shots not taken. Don't focus on why you can't do something. Instead, just start where you are with what you have. Because in the end, it's the greatest challenges that also make the greatest stories and strongest heroes.

As Pastor Alex Himaya, the international speaker, author, and senior pastor of theChurch.at, told me during our interview, "Too terribly often, young people over-evaluate the future and under appreciate what they can do today."

When God calls you, start right where you are with what's in your hand—whether it's a sling, an idea, or a GoPro—and dare to venture into the wild. Because in the end, yes, faith is dangerous. But the alternative is routine, and routine is lethal.

Through the Storm

Breathing deeply, I tried to focus on the music blasting through my vehicle speakers. It was January of 2015, putting me at just over 100 interviews, and I was driving home from Oklahoma City after a long, productive day of five different hour-long interviews I'd done with influential leaders around OKC.

The sun had just dropped below the horizon, so while the eastern half of the sky had already turned black due to the storm clouds covering it, the western edge of the sky still glowed with intense orange and yellow as the final rays of sunlight cut through the thunderheads. In anticipation of the big storm about to hit, there was already a light drizzle wafting through the air. The moisture collecting on my windshield soon pooled into water droplets that reflected the bright lights of the city surrounding me on both sides.

I had just merged onto the interstate toward my house and was listening to music through the stereo at full blast in an attempt to drown out my thoughts and emotions of the day and stay calm. But suddenly, at the flip of a switch, the music lost its hypnotic effect on me and all the emotions I had been suppressing throughout the day instantly came crashing down on me in an overwhelming heap.

My composure snapped, and I let out a long, exhaustive yell at the top of my lungs into the closed interior of my vehicle. But this wasn't enough to satisfy the burning rage, pain, and fear welling up inside me that demanded to be released. I frantically lowered my window, letting the still lightweight and intermittent raindrops pelt me in the face. Then I let loose another exhaustive scream into the cold, whipping wind now rushing through my open window.

You might be wondering what kind of terrible event must have occurred to evoke this kind of response from me. The fact is, it was nothing.

Not a thing had happened that day out of the ordinary. I'd spent my day doing interviews, taking notes, meeting people, making phone calls, and road tripping, and as far as a productive day goes, I had killed it. Yet driving home, I felt completely empty, like I had forgotten what I was doing and why I was doing it.

Truth be told, I actually had forgotten why. I'd forgotten why I'd set out on this journey, I'd lost sight of my dream, and I was stuck in nothing more than a routine. For the past month, I'd been trying to compensate for my lack of vision by being extremely productive, subconsciously hoping that meaningless results could fill the void left by my lack of purpose. It hadn't worked.

Driving home from OKC that night with my wet hair whipping in the cold winter wind and my mouth torn wide open in scream after scream, I vented my outrage at God. There wasn't anyone else around to yell at, and besides, God was the one who had led me down this stupid path in the first place. *"Do 500 interviews?* I thought. *Yeah, right. What even for?"* I had no idea.

I remembered back to the passion I'd caught soon after the

beginning of my project. I'd been on a God-orchestrated mission to question reality and find truth. Where had that drive gone? The daily passion-filled and desire-driven grind I used to relish had vanished, replaced with a mundane single-mindedness that said: "Go interview people because that's what you did yesterday." Somehow, over time I had become so wrapped up in what I was doing that I had forgotten why I was doing it.

At that moment I felt tempted to dive into a barrage of self-motivation, to blast music and let my chest reverberate with sound, to smack a broad grin on my face and convince myself I was fine. But I didn't have the energy. How does one even rekindle their dream after they've let it burn out? I didn't know the answer to that, either.

Eventually, all my breath was spent and my voice hurt, so I stopped yelling, slumped against my car door, and started trembling with exhaustion. I was a mess. I noticed tears were running down my face and then mingling with the raindrops still pelting me. However, I couldn't tell if I was crying because of my swelling emotions or because of the cold wind biting my face. Probably a combination of both.

My gaze became a blank stare, and with nowhere else to turn, I turned to the one I'd been screaming at for the past ten minutes. I tried to pray with words in my head, but my mind was too frantic to keep straight thoughts. So instead, I let loose my emotions and prayed with feelings.

I don't know how long I drove circles outside Oklahoma City, but finally, I managed to regain some composure. I wiped my forearm across my face to clear my eyes of the tears and rainwater obscuring my vision. If only clearing the vision of your heart and soul were so easy. The monstrous question *"Why?"* still loomed over me, feeling a thousand times bigger than the storm clouds covering the sky. *"Why am I doing this?"* I asked myself.

I didn't know, so I thought back to the time when I *had* known— the time after I'd talked with Lecrae five months ago. Of course, it hadn't been Lecrae himself who had given me that sense of purpose.

No, the sense of purpose I'd gained had been due to the prayer I'd prayed: *"Father, give me a second chance…"*

Somehow, when I had prayed that prayer, the words had melded to my mind and sealed all the cracks in my resolve, preventing any more of it from leaking out. God had given me a second chance, and I'd taken it, committing that I would find the answer to my childhood question if it killed me.

Now, as I remembered that prayer, I asked myself a question. God had given me a vision. He'd given me talents. He'd given me opportunities. He'd given me this whole crazy project. So, what was I going to do with it all?

With the faint mental strength I had left, I answered myself: *"Everything I can."*

That was as specific as I could make my answer, but it was enough. My panic faded away, and a shaky strength returned to my mind. I got bearings on what road I was on and started working my way home. I was already soaking wet, so I didn't see any point in rolling the window up—the water rolling down my face made me feel awake, anyway.

What was the point of this? I still wasn't entirely sure, but I knew that God knew what the point was, and I trusted him. Maybe he'd show me someday.

Driving home from OKC, sputtering rainwater and crying like a little boy, I learned a lesson I'll always remember: never forget why. Once you're alive with purpose, your greatest threat is not the challenges and dangers that stand in your way, but that complacency and routine might rid you of the fire it takes to fight those challenges and brave the dangers. We've got to remember why, or the "what" and "how" will serve us no good.

Like Jeff Osborne, a prison convict turned evangelist and motivational speaker from California, later told me when I asked him about how to maintain passion in your heart even through the tough times, "Remember why you started, and remember the prayers you prayed."

Embrace It

Without passion, what more is life than mere existence? Passion is why we care. Passion is why we bother. Passion is why we fight on. Passion is why we get back up. Passion is the fire in our veins. I used to think passion was something special that only certain people were born with, but since then, I've learned the truth. As Wes Lane, the founder of a Christ-purposed leadership network in OKC called SALLT, once told me, "Everyone has an ember in their heart, and to come alive, all you have to do is fan it."

God made you with innate dreams and convictions, and passion starts flaming when you start living those out. If there's something you believe in or dream of, have the guts to fight for it even though others might doubt you. Refuse to listen to fear.

If there's something you hate, have the backbone to stand against it and hold your ground even though some people may dislike you for it. Refuse to listen to fear. Stop hiding from the battle you feel called to fight. Tear fear apart and stay true to who you are by chasing your dreams and fighting for what you believe in.

As *Duck Dynasty*'s Sadie Robertson told me in our interview, "Being yourself and fulfilling the calling God has given you at the time is a lot like what a physical trainer will tell you when working out: listen to your body."

It took me longer than I would have liked to learn it, but Sadie's dead right. Listen to your body, listen to your spirit, listen to your heart, and go. Start with who you know you are, and as you continue to stay true to that and push yourself, you'll discover who you're made to be. But this does require you to take risks, to push yourself, and to be vulnerable. Like the stallion trainer Lew Sterrett once told me, "You will never find yourself by protecting yourself."

Stoke your fire in accord with who you are, but not in accord with what feels comfortable. A lesson Chris Goede, vice president of the John Maxwell company, shared with me is, "Stay in your gift zone, get out of your comfort zone."

Face the challenges, brave the danger, and embrace the struggle. Embrace the pain of growth. Embrace feeling sore. Embrace it all, because when you do, the person God made you to be will start to emerge from beneath all the comfort you've covered yourself in. As Charlie Hall, the renowned Christian music songwriter, would tell me, "Embrace the pain, brokenness, and chaos. It rips off the fake."

The deal with passion is that it only stays so long as you keep moving. Every fire is either growing or dying, and so while you should never be someone you're not, you should also never accept where you are. You'll turn to ash if you do. What God has given us is not ours for consumption, but for propulsion.

Like Calvin Burgess, a Christian business tycoon who followed God's calling on his life to be a missionary by instituting an enormous agricultural company in Africa, told me, "Everyone is called, but few answer the call. Certainly, I could spend the rest of my life kicked back on a beach or yacht somewhere. I thought about it once, but then God asked me, 'If that's all you plan to do with your life and with all I've given you, then why did I train you?'"

Dare to dream, but don't stop there. Dare to let go of security and abandon routine. Stop trying to protect who you appear to be, and start becoming who you were made to be. Dream, and dare to chase the call.

Adventure > Ease

In summer of 2015, my family took the vacation of a lifetime to Hawaii. At the time I was right in the middle of the 500 interviews and was keen on maintaining interview progress even while on vacation. So, with the help of a friend of ours from Hawaii, Mark Button, I managed to get connected with Kaimana Plemer, the founder of the lifestyle brand HE>i ("He is greater than I").

Having grown up on the North Shore of Oahu, immersed in surf culture, Kaimana has a wild story. Back in 2003, he had just purchased a new phone and wanted a cool, original screen saver. Based on the

Bible verse John 3:30, "He must become greater; I must become less" (NIV), he chose the headline "HE>i," and others noticed. Pretty soon, he was spraying the symbol-turned-lifestyle-logo on T-shirts and printing it on stickers. It quickly caught on as an original, shorthand way of expressing one's Christian faith and as a conversation starter with others.

Kaimana and I spent an hour talking on the porch outside the HE>i store in Haleiwa, Oahu, and one of the things I remember he told me about starting his brand was this: "We didn't want to be stuck inside Christian bookstores. We wanted to be part of the surf shops and culture we grew up fascinated with. But, integrating ourselves into the shops that already existed didn't work because of our conflicting message. So, we decided to set out on our own and do it our own way."

It took time for me to realize it, but one thing I later learned from that conversation is that a dream mutilated by and conformed to "reality" isn't really a dream anymore, but a chore. When you let your dream be diminished by and molded to the way things are and what everyone else says it should be, you lose the passion for it and it's not yours anymore. If you give up ownership of your dream in order to avoid a challenge, you'll come to regret it—because in the end, you'll come to realize that the adventure you found in your dream was worth far more to you than whatever amount of ease or money you sold it for.

It's stories like Kaimana's that have brought me to understand that while you always have to start where you are, you should never accept where you are. Most people think that challenges, problems, and difficulties are hindrances to their dream, but in fact, overcoming those challenges is the very essence of what makes the story worth telling in the end. That's one way you can know a worthwhile dream apart from an empty one: is it bigger than the challenges you face?

Heat comes from the friction of wood against wood, and passion comes from the friction of desire against challenge. If you forfeit part of your desire in order to remove part of the challenge, you take away both parts of what it takes to make a dream worthwhile, so never downgrade. If you can't figure out how to make your dream work where you are, don't minimize it. Don't let circumstances determine the story you tell. If your dream doesn't fit into your circumstances—which it probably won't—then dream bigger than your circumstances, and *you* decide what story you tell.

Sacred Responsibility

As you're reading this book, I don't want you to get the impression that this idea of sold-out, "go big or go home", bet-the-farm risk-taking approach to life is just the outpouring of an overly adventurous teenager and his fantasies. Trust me, I definitely am a teenager with a thirst for adventure, and if not for God having changed me from the inside out, I never would have bothered to write this book.

This isn't an overflow of me, but of what God has filled me with and what I've learned from warriors and leaders of God's kingdom. Though not all are "famous", every single one of the people I've talked with is definitely *influential*, and all are maximizing their lives to make a difference in the world.

From Esther to David to the disciples to Jesus himself, no warrior of God I know of ever stepped into their calling and completed their mission with a half-hearted, timid approach to life. Even the "parable of the talents" in the Bible (Matthew 25:14-30) makes it clear that the gifts and opportunities God gives us are entrusted to us for His glory and for us to do something with. And if we don't do something with them, they'll be taken away from us.

It's not our privilege to invest and maximize everything God entrusts to us—it's our *responsibility*. The kingdom of God demands passion and initiative. Jeff Osborne, the Californian pastor I mentioned earlier, told me, "When you get who we represent and that the kingdom of God demands aggression, you also realize that passivity is not an option."

Not only do I see it as my responsibility to maximize the impact of my life for the kingdom of God, but I'm also disgusted with the idea of settling for any lesser prospect. I don't believe that when God calls us to His purpose He demands "just enough"—I believe he demands *everything*.

Every dream and passion God has breathed into you, he's given to you for a reason. Fulfilling your calling in life isn't as much about accomplishing one thing you're called to do as it is simply bringing the light, love, and hope of Christ to people in everything you do, and bringing it to the highest intensity. Like Wayne Simmonds, the Canadian professional hockey player, told me, "Prioritize God in everything you do. We can get caught up in work, in our hobbies, in whatever, and forget that our calling is to make it *all* for His glory. It's all sacred."

Be faithful with the little God has given you, and he will entrust you with more than you could ever imagine.

Chapter 3

THE CORE

"To anyone who wants to be part of the film industry, here's my question: what would it take to make you give up? To make you quit? If there's an answer to that question, you won't make it."

—Jon Erwin,
film director, interview #497

Pacing back in forth in my dad's study, I briefly rehearsed a monologue in my head. It was July of 2015, and I was about to reach out to Willie Robertson, the bearded CEO TV star of *Duck Dynasty*. The evident strength of Willie's character and the way he used his influence and success to make a difference for Christ had always drawn me to him. Ever since the beginning of my project, I had known I would someday reach out to him with a request for a meeting. Today was finally that day.

With a final self-affirmation of my monologue, I retrieved my phone from where I'd set it on a table and navigated to a phone number I had saved. My plan was to call the Robertson family business, Duck Commander, of which Willie was the CEO, ask the receptionist for help connecting with Willie, and follow whatever lead I was given.

Easy-peasy. Excitement and enthusiasm thundered through my body as I hit 'call,' making my skin tingle with keen sensation.

"Thank you for calling Duck Commander, this is Lynda! How can I help you?" the receptionist greeted me warmly.

I calmly explained myself and before I knew it, I was forwarded to one of the company's executive assistants to further discuss my request for an interview. *Sweet.* Thing's were already going better than I'd hoped.

After a few rings, I reached the assistant's voicemail. I would have preferred to have had the conversation in real time, but I didn't mind leaving a message. I stated my name and began sharing about my project in preparation for asking for a meeting with Willie—and that's when everything went south.

About halfway through leaving my voicemail, my voice started faltering as I became short of breath. I hardly noticed at first, but before long I could barely get a sentence out of my mouth before I had to gasp for air. *"What in the world is wrong with me?"* I thought. My tongue felt like sandpaper as I started rambling and stumbling over my words. I began to panic. What I felt was a solid first step toward connecting with Willie quickly turned into a nightmare as I continued to gasp for air between each word I spoke.

Then things got worse.

Because of my short breath, I was becoming frantic, horrified of the voicemail I was leaving and also freaking out that I might be becoming asthmatic. As a result, I was so distracted by my trouble breathing that I dragged the voicemail out much longer than it needed to be.

"Your voicemail time has expired," said the automated voice before it beeped and disconnected me. I froze, my phone limp in my hand, my mouth still open in mid-sentence. Suddenly, my previous feeling of passionate excitement was replaced by intense dread.

I couldn't believe this was actually happening. I had already done over 250 interviews and was honestly getting pretty good. I knew my introductory monologue forward and backward and could say it in my sleep. What was going on?

I paused for a second and tried to recapture my breath, still unsure of why I couldn't breathe properly, and then called the Duck Commander assistant back. Getting her voicemail again, I gave a pitiful apology for the message I had just left, tried to summarize my goal clearly and quickly, and just barely managed to say my number and email address before I came up short of breath again.

As I turned off my phone, I walked into our family living room and sunk into the couch, wanting to hide from the world. I felt like a kid who had just wet his pants in front of all his friends.

A few days later, I got an email back from the assistant. I didn't get the interview.

I could hardly believe it was all real. I had never failed at an interview request so miserably before. I'd made an absolute fool of myself. I would have been better off not reaching out to Willie at all—or, that's how I felt at first.

Despite the terrible disappointment and waves of nausea that washed over me for months after that incident, I learned several things from that day I called Duck Commander. First of all, it didn't take me long to realize that the reason I'd been short of breath hadn't been because I was experiencing an asthma attack. Rather, my sinuses had been stuffy and it had been hard for me to breathe while talking so much. But I also learned something a whole lot more important.

In the weeks that followed, the failure I experienced in trying to reach out to Willie didn't deter me at all. In fact, my intensity only continued to increase after that experience—not the giddy excitement and enthusiasm I'd experienced just before calling Willie, which had been extinguished immediately afterward, but something burning far deeper inside me. At the core of who I was, something drove me forward even after my surface-level symptoms of excitement and enthusiasm had been temporarily knocked out.

It would take time before I fully understood what that "something" was, but what I've come to learn since then is that excitement and enthusiasm are like gasoline: they can keep your passion burning for a while, but if your *resolve* at the core of who you are never catches fire, your passion will soon burn out.

Uncomfortable

When I first began my interviews project, I had dreamed of it being one of the most passionate and adventurous journeys I'd ever gone on, which it was. However, it was incidents like the day I reached out to Willie that continually showed me it would also be one of the most grueling and difficult challenges I'd ever fought through.

For me, the hardest part of my project wasn't making progress. From conducting interviews to planning road trips, the things I had to do were usually pretty simple to accomplish. The hard part was simply that there was *soooo* much progress that had to be made.

In the end, I pulled through most of my journey in the same way Admiral Kirk Hinnrichs of the United States Coast Guard told me during our interview he had pulled through in his own life: "I'm not where I am today because I'm the smartest, and I don't think I worked the hardest, but I did put myself in positions that no one else would, and I held on the longest."

The truth is, if you refuse to lose in your mind, you'll eventually win in reality.

Growing up, one lesson my dad never failed to stress to me was that, "Everyone pays in life: you either pay now and play later, or play now and pay forever." In other words, if you grit your teeth and conquer what's hard right now, you'll eventually be able to achieve what was once impossible because you're becoming stronger.

But if you slack off and mess around right now, you'll pay the consequence indefinitely because the problem won't lie in the difficulty of life—which constantly changes—but rather, in the fact that you've let yourself grow weak—which only you can change. As Cody Bobay, a former active duty Naval Aircrewman and now founder of the men's ministry Soulcon told me during our interview, "Nothing gets easier—you get tougher."

Dumbbells don't get lighter. You get stronger, and not lifting them only makes you weaker. Cliff jumping doesn't get less frightening. You get braver, and not jumping only makes you more afraid.

It's uncomfortable to lift weights, it's uncomfortable to cliff jump, and it's uncomfortable to test your limits. But to become more of who you're made to be, you have to push yourself into the uncomfortable.

Living a passionate and on-fire life requires grit and determination just as much as it requires enthusiasm and excitement, and it requires getting uncomfortable. Trevor Williams, a Life.Church campus pastor in Oklahoma, told me, "We should find comfort in our faith, but it should never make us comfortable."

Real strength doesn't come from your stuff or success, but from who you are inside. As Dennis Peacocke, a Californian speaker, author, and the founder of the Christ-focused leadership organization GoStrategic, told me, "Practice doesn't make perfect, it makes preeminence. And what I practice I eventually become."

The truth of those words rings the same on both ends of the spectrum: if you practice being weak and scared, that's who you'll become, and if you practice being strong and brave, that's who you'll become. It's through every opportunity and challenge you encounter in life that you further define which one it will be. For instance…

Autographs

A month after my cringing phone call to Willie Robertson, my dad and I were at the Catalyst Conference, an annual event for evangelical leaders, pastors, and entrepreneurs held in Atlanta, Georgia.

On the first day of the event, I found myself in a room listening to an interview of Andy Mineo, a Christian rapper and hip-hop artist from New York who I'm a big fan of. All the chairs in the room were taken, as well as any spaces against the walls, so I'd taken to the floor.

I hadn't seen Andy in person since I was probably twelve or thirteen years old when I'd gone to a youth concert of his with some friends.

After the interview, Andy said he was going to be signing his new album, *Uncomfortable*, outside. At first, I thought to myself I would just try to talk with Andy another time when the two of us could actually have a real conversation. I thought talking with him now in an album signing was going to be too generic and predictable of a way to meet him for the first time.

But recalling the time I'd stood in line to talk with Dr. Ben Carson, I shot that thought down fast. I decided that while I definitely wanted to try to have a real conversation with Andy later on as well, I was going to seize the moment and talk with him during the album signing first. With my mind made up, I scrambled to my feet, rushed to the table selling his new album, and got in line for the signing as fast as possible.

While in line to talk with Andy, I noticed everyone in front of me was taking selfies with him, asking him to sign their copy of his new album, and then moving on. No one was talking with him much at all. Because the line was moving so quickly I didn't want to take more time than I felt I was due, so when I got to Andy, I said, "Hey, Andy! My name's Holden. Can I trade my picture with you for a question?"

"Sure!" he said. "Let's hear it!"

After briefly sharing about my project, I asked him for his advice on how, as young people, we should train and prepare ourselves to better lead and make a difference as we grow older. He paused in signing my copy of his album, obviously thinking about the question, and then said, "It's big, but it's simple. It's the spiritual disciplines: prayer, being in the Word, relationships; all of those things. If you do those things, you will be trained for whatever it is, because those trainings apply across the board."

I thanked Andy with a broad smile and told him I hoped to talk with him again soon. In my mind, my plan was to contact Andy's agency after the conference and ask for a follow-up conversation with him.

With that, I stepped out of line to a nearby wall, pressed my back against it, and let myself slide to the floor where I opened my leather-bound journal to a blank page. Hurriedly, I scribbled the heading "ANDY MINEO — INTERVIEW" onto the page and Andy's quote beneath it. It was sloppily written, but I didn't care; the print didn't need to be pretty for me to remember this crazy experience. And boy, was my day just getting started!

A few hours after my conversation with Andy Mineo, I was given another opportunity to talk with a different Andy, this one far more intimidating to me: Andy Stanley, the senior pastor at North Point Community Church at campuses throughout the metro Atlanta area, as well as a leadership author, speaker, and guru for other pastors, entrepreneurs, and leaders. Andy Stanley had just given a talk in the massive auditorium of Catalyst and it had then been announced he was going to hold a book signing outside.

"Album and book signings…" I thought to myself sarcastically, rolling my eyes. I still found it a little ridiculous that I was being forced to stoop as low as "book signings" to find interview opportunities. But after my previous encounter with Andy Mineo, my pride had been leveled a little bit. *"I guess you start where you are with what you have,"* I reminded myself.

A few minutes later, I found myself in a line yet again, holding what I considered an "Andy Stanley conversation token"—his book *Next Generation Leader.* It felt very similar to Andy Mineo's album signing line I'd been in earlier that day, except that this time, I felt terribly nervous.

As a matter of fact, the fear churning my mind had grown so rampant that it had disbanded any previous thoughts I'd had on my distaste for "book signing interviews." I was breathing so hard that my dad, who was in line beside me, even sarcastically remarked, "Holden, are you okay? You don't want to scare Andy off when you get up there to him."

And that was it exactly—because as it turned out, throughout my project Andy Stanley had so far eluded me. Over the past year, I had tried to connect with Andy several times before for an interview but had been turned down every time. On one particular occasion several months earlier, Andy Stanley had been part of conducting a one-day leadership training conference in Tulsa, Oklahoma, that I had opted not to attend in favor of something else I had going.

During that conference, a family friend of ours had even mentioned me and my project to Andy directly to ask if he would be interested in talking with me for a few minutes sometime. However, when Andy had heard I wanted to talk with him but hadn't even come to the conference, it had been a deal breaker. I was told his response had been, "If this kid wanted to learn about leadership from me, he should have been in the conference auditorium taking notes." In the end, I guess he's right.

Nonetheless, I was pretty sure once I eventually reached Andy at the book signing and told him I was on a mission to meet and learn from 500 Christian leaders, he would remember me and be willing to give me at least a brief minute to include him in my project. At least, that's what I was trying to tell myself.

I even thought maybe I could joke about being "the kid who didn't show up to his conference." But my secret fear was that Andy wouldn't find it amusing at all and wouldn't have changed his mind. I even worried Andy might have me removed from the book signing once he learned who I was. Ridiculous, I know, but true nonetheless.

With these concerns swirling in my mind, the fear in me started coming up with every possible excuse as to why I should get out of line right then and just be glad to watch Andy on stage. I wasn't prepared. These were bad circumstances. Andy probably didn't want to talk with me. He'd surely already heard and previously answered any question I could come up with. I was no one.

Before I knew it, I was only a couple of people away from him, and I still didn't feel prepared or know what to say or how to say it. This was most definitely not the way I had dreamed of talking with Andy Stanley. But as much as I truly did want to step out of line right then, resolve kept my feet planted. It refused to let me run. A part of me—the part that cared—knew this opportunity would likely be the only chance I would have to talk with Andy before the end of my 500 interviews.

When I finally got to Andy, I introduced myself with as much confidence as I could summon and briefly summarized my project as if I thought he had never heard of it before: "I'm a seventeen-year-old on a mission to meet and learn from 500 different Christian leaders across the country." Then I asked him my question.

As best I recall, my question had something to do with the message Andy had delivered earlier that day, mashed together with "what it took to pioneer" and "how to make a difference." Honestly, it was a clumsy question for the nervousness swirling inside of me, and I really don't remember what exactly I asked—but I'll always remember the response I got.

I'm honestly not sure that Andy even remembered he'd heard about my project before; if he did put the two together, he didn't show it. Instead, after I finished rambling, he moved straight to answering my question, and in my panicked state, that was definitely alright with me.

He said, "Take advantage of every opportunity that comes your way. That's it. And if you aren't sure about it, try it anyway. If you fail, so what? You're seventeen."

I thanked him, half of my mind ecstatic at what I'd just accomplished and the other half relieved that the ordeal was over. As I had done after my conversation with Andy Mineo, I immediately walked to the nearest wall, slid to the floor with my open journal, and made note of Andy Stanley's quote underneath a headline stating his name in bold, all-caps print. Then, for the first time that day, I finally had a moment to think.

Deeper

I felt different. Of course, don't we all feel different after we face our fears? Almost like we're suddenly engulfed in freedom. The freedom to try something even if we might fail. That's the feeling I felt, as I had many times before. But this time, I allowed myself the time to process and think through what had just happened.

One of the crazy things about all this for me was that Andy Stanley's words had directly reinforced what I had gone through to hear him say them. We try, we fail, we try again, fail again, and try again, and eventually, the only thing that can happen is we grow stronger and eventually succeed. That's exactly what I had done.

The week after Catalyst, I tried to follow through with my plan to earn a follow-up conversation with Andy Mineo, the rapper. I contacted Reach Records, shared my project in more compelling detail, said I'd met Andy Mineo at his Catalyst album signing, and asked if I could have a little more time to talk with him. In the end, his team loved my project and what I was doing but had to tell me that Andy simply didn't have time.

I was disappointed, of course, but not regretful. No, not regretful at all, because I had tried. The fact is, I could've waited for the perfect opportunity, but if I had, I would have missed any opportunity at all.

I remember meeting with Pastor Mark Batterson, international speaker and bestselling author of the *Circle Maker,* in Washington, DC, and taking note of something he said that I'll never forget: "At the end of your life, your greatest regrets will be the opportunities you missed. It's the inaction regrets, neglected opportunities, and risks you *didn't* take. Something you didn't do that you could have or should have done."

Most people think that the secret to living without regrets is never messing up and never failing, but actually, it's just the opposite. In life, there are two kinds of pain: action pain and inaction pain. Action pain comes from the growth of boldness, while inaction pain comes from the regret of cowardice. The difference between the two is that action pain makes us stronger and eventually fades into scars on our skin as our bodies heal, while inaction pain tears us apart from inside our heart like a parasite and few people ever really free themselves of it.

Every time we have a dream, every time we are faced with a challenge, and every time we feel our heart calling us, we have the choice to either engage the adventure and *try* or to stay where it's safe and hide. That decision right there will determine whether you eventually grow strong and brave, or weak and scared.

Like Larry Bross, the executive director of Oklahoma's poverty-fighting ministry City Care, told me, "Don't ever give up. Don't quit. If you quit, the next time you want to quit it will be a little bit easier, and the next time easier still, until eventually you're nothing but a quitter."

I've learned the opposite is also true. Never give up. Don't quit. The next time you want to quit because you're tired or because you're in pain, keep going and fight on, and the next time you want to quit, grit your teeth and fight on. Eventually, you'll be a champion.

What many people don't realize is that there's a difference between failure and defeat. Failure is what happens when you mess up, but defeat is what happens when you quit on yourself. In fact, messing up is a basic part of what it takes to achieve success because really, it's by failing that we learn and grow better.

Failure is the teacher and pain is the tuition price. It's taken me a long time to realize it, but what I've finally come to see is that if you never risk more than you know you can already do, you will never become more than you already are. As financial guru Dave Ramsey told me, "Success is a mountain of failure; just instead of people lying underneath it, they're standing on top of it."

Everyone makes mistakes, but not everyone makes progress. That's where the deeper level of passion is born. Everyone's journey in life eventually becomes rough and exhausting, but only a few are willing to take the punches of failure and get back up. Are you?

When continuing the journey no longer feels warm and exciting, does your passion reach deep enough for you to fight on? The *feeling* of passion can be enough to fuel us for a while, but if it never becomes something deeper than that, someday it won't be enough. Eventually, passion has to become part of your character, not just temporary hype, or you'll burn out.

Iron Bones

How strong are you? Deeper than the success you have, the money in your bank account, the power you've accumulated, the comfort you've covered yourself in, the illusions of safety you've placed around yourself, and even the passion your saturated in, how strong are *you?* The "you" that remains even when chaos tears everything else away? The "you" at the core?

It's not a question that many of us ever think about. We strive to strengthen the extensions of ourselves—the engines we operate and tools we use such as our jobs, our businesses, our careers, our plans, our reputations, and our charisma. But in the process, we fail to strengthen the most important thing of all: our character.

I remember champion horse trainer Lew Sterrett once shared with me that, "People don't rise to the occasion; they fall to their level of preparation."

With every opportunity or challenge I encounter in life, the truth of Lew's statement continues to be driven further home to me. People don't rise to the occasion—they fall to their level of preparation. They fall to the strength of their character. They fall to the core of who they are. When the occasion demands you to be strong beyond what you're surface-level excitement and enthusiasm can supply, you will either fall to the resolve burning deep inside you or fall right through where your resolve should have been—to the defeat lurking beneath.

I learned this first-hand in November of 2015 when I arrived with my family at an event at the National Cowboy Hall of Fame in Oklahoma City. Normally, I would have been ramping myself up in anticipation for an aggressive night of networking and meeting people worth including in my project. But as it was, I had just recently gotten home from my trip to Atlanta and was mentally worn out, so I had decided to take it easy and just enjoy the night without trying to work the event. Or so I thought.

Mere minutes after arriving on the scene, I discovered the guest speaker for the event was former First Lady Laura Bush, wife of President George W. Bush. Cool enough, right? But that wasn't it. As it turned out, Mrs. Bush was having a reception, and my family was going to get to have our picture taken with her.

With an exhausted shrug of my shoulders, I put my tired mind behind myself and set my jaw, knowing what I had to do: make a way for me to talk with Mrs. Bush. I had to do it, because that was what interviewing 500 incredible people took. There was no excited glint in my eyes. No exuberance emanating from my voice. No surface-level passion prickled across my skin. But beneath the surface and behind my tired eyes, a deeper-set passion stirred inside me like a quiet storm.

Standing in line to meet Laura thirty minutes later, my mind was in whirring motion, thinking of how I could briefly "interview" her. Boy, by this time ABS&R (album/book signing and reception) opportunities were becoming killer. I noticed the procession was moving extremely fast, with people barely having enough time to shake Mrs. Bush's hand before the next group was ushered in for a picture.

It occurred to me that yet again, I would have time for only one question. And as I continued to watch the line, I began to doubt I would even have the time for that.

When we got to Mrs. Bush, my mom and dad managed to shake her hand before her team grouped us around her for a picture and then started ushering us out of the line. Honestly, if this had been before I'd started the interviews, I would have followed the flow of traffic and moved right along without having even said a thing to Mrs. Bush—and even now, the situation taunted my tired mind with legitimate excuses to bypass my efforts entirely.

Part of me wanted to give up and let myself break, to forfeit talking with Mrs. Bush and just follow the flow, but I couldn't. Resolve steeled my body like iron in my bones.

Just as the last of my family exited the photo set, I stopped in my tracks, turned to Mrs. Bush, and introduced myself before her team could stop me. One of her bodyguards, the one who had ushered the rest of my family out of the photo set, started barking at me to move along, but I was already committed.

As I briefly explained my project to Mrs. Bush, I used my peripheral vision to keep tabs on the bodyguard, mildly concerned he might come grab me from behind the neck and throw me out. I finished my spiel and question to Mrs. Bush, who then nodded with a smile before offering her simple but profound answer: "You can learn so much by listening to others and by receiving what they have to offer. And of course, by reading the Word."

I smiled broadly, dipped my head, and extending my hand one last time to shake hers, said, "Thank you so much Mrs. Bush!" Knowing Laura Bush was a former teacher and librarian with a passion for literacy, I especially appreciated her response. But for me, the biggest impact of that entire scenario was realizing I could push through something even when I didn't feel like doing so.

One of the things Doug Carter, the Senior Vice President of EQUIP Leadership (a branch of John Maxwell's leadership organization) told me during our interview was, "If you're really good at making excuses, you won't be any good at anything else." In life, excuses will always be there, and often they're usually at least somewhat valid. So you have to decide: Do you want to grow strong, or grow comfortable?

It's up to you, because in the end, excuses will only hold you back to the degree your resolve is weak.

Chapter 4

LEAD

"Everyone becomes someone. Who you become is either up to you or up to someone else."

—Rex Crain,
motivational speaker, interview #477

With deliberate, calm breaths, I surveyed my situation, first glancing down at the ground forty feet below me and then at the rope and climbing harness secured around my waist. It was December of 2016, and some friends of mine and I were visiting our local rock climbing gym. Built around repurposed grain silos, the gym's ninety-foot-high exterior is covered in graffiti-style artwork while the interior is outfitted with a large array of climbing routes. It's one of those routes I was now attempting to scale.

My friend Ryan was belaying me from down on the ground, and at my request, she was also timing my ascent. By my count, I was probably forty-five seconds into my climb and had finally reached a point on the wall where I was forced to stop and plot my next move.

Rather than continuing straight up, the route now veered sharply to the right for the next couple yards and was speckled with small finger-niche holds that I knew would take my amateur self a considerable amount of time to cross. I normally would have already started working my way across the finger niche section. Considering that I was in a race against the clock, however, I found myself searching for a faster route than the obvious one in front of me.

I took another glance at my predicament, aware that I'd already burned several seconds doing nothing. Then, as I glanced to the other side of the route, my second option became apparent to me.

I quickly chalked my hands up in anticipation of executing my plan, finding that I was now suddenly nervous. Experienced climbers would probably laugh at my fear, but what I was plotting sure wasn't a laughing matter for me. I knew the harness around my waist would catch me if my plan ended badly. Nonetheless, the subconscious part of my mind that operated out of survival instinct now scrambled for control of my body as the consciously reasoning part of my mind schemed of risk. With mental effort, I did my best to channel the fear I felt into excitement, and then proceeded.

Letting the chalk bag fall to my side, I flexed my body left to give myself swinging room, like pulling back the drawstring on a bow before releasing the arrow. I focused my gaze on a large handhold a few yards to my right on the other side of the finger niche holds. Then, without a moment's more hesitation, I launched myself upward and to the right, jumping across the entire section of the climb in front of me and managing to latch hold of my target grip on the other side with my right hand. It was a good hold, and in a flash I pulled myself up.

Proud of myself and happy to be on a roll again, I smiled and finished my race to the top of the route. But that first climb was just the beginning for me.

An hour later, Ryan and I had migrated to another climb, this one significantly taller than the first and far more arduous. Ryan was belaying me again when, at about ten minutes into my climb, my forearms began to fatigue. I decided to take a break in order to rest and regain my grip strength.

I started climbing again, but in no time at all, my arms once more felt like noodles and I was forced to stop for another break. The third time my grip strength went out, I thought, *"That's it, I'm done"* and yelled down at Ryan to lower me.

"No," she yelled back up at me, *"You can do this!"*

I opened my mouth and took in a breath of air in order to yell back at her that I really was done, but something stopped me. In the back of my mind, I knew she was right—I wasn't done, my body just wanted to be.

So, choosing to lead my own mind rather than follow what was easy, I stretched my forearms out and started climbing again. The lactic acid now pumping through my muscles made my arms burn, but I pressed on, and though my body hurt, the fight to make it to the top made me feel incredibly alive.

After finally reaching the top of my climb, now nearly 100 feet above the ground, I remembered something again that I'd learned many times before: to climb higher, whether on a rock wall or in life, following the flow won't get you there.

If you simply wait to drift to the top as you flow with the currents of safety and ease, there's one undeniable law of physics that will keep you from ever making it: gravity. The currents of safety and ease, like the currents of water, only flow downhill. The only way up is to fight the current—and to do that, you have to *lead* yourself.

On Purpose

No one ever just stumbles into "awesome." People don't just wake up one day and find themselves a gold medal-winning Olympic athlete. Weights don't lift themselves, miles don't run themselves, and limits don't push themselves. For me, I've learned pretty clearly that rock walls don't climb themselves.

To go somewhere awesome you have to lead yourself there, because, like David Green, founder of the arts-and-crafts chain of Hobby Lobby superstores once told me, "Vision without discipline and hard work doesn't go anywhere."

Dreams without action are dead, and actions without a dream are lost; it takes both to move forward. In the end, the truth is that dreams don't take you somewhere—*you* take you somewhere. Dreams are just the direction. As my pastor, Craig Groeschel, would say, "Everyone ends up somewhere, but few people end up somewhere on purpose."

Few people decide where they want to end up and intentionally go there. Most people just let themselves drift with the crowd and simply end up wherever the current drops them. The problem I've learned with drifting, though, is that currents only flow downhill, so when you drift with the crowd, you also drain into the sewer with them.

Funny, isn't it then, that normal crowd-following people are always complaining about how bad it stinks where they are. The fact is, if you want to climb the mountain, following the crowd won't get you there—you have to lead yourself there.

Most people think of a leader as someone who is in charge, but I don't believe that's true. It certainly can be true, because authority often comes with being a leader, but it's not what makes someone a leader. As my friend Anna Groeschel once told me, "You can't lead others without first leading yourself."

It's a misunderstanding that leaders only lead and don't follow, because really, I've found that leaders are the truest followers to exist. Leaders follow their beliefs, their dreams, their gut, other leaders they look up to, and the calling God has given them. You cannot lead others toward something you aren't chasing yourself.

If there's a crowd of thousands behind you, but you aren't chasing anything, you aren't leading; you merely happen to be in front of everyone as you all drift in the same direction. The difference between followers and leaders isn't that one follows and the other doesn't; the difference is in what they're following.

So what do you follow? The crowd, or your heart? That is the difference between followers and leaders, and it's up to you which one you will be, because people make the switch from follower to leader when they stop being dragged and they start pulling.

Lead

Better Than I Deserve

With the morning sun just breaking over the horizon and asphalt blurring beneath our family's pickup as I sped down the road, I looked down at the navigation on my phone: twelve more hours to go until arriving in Nashville, Tennessee. It had only been an hour since I'd left home, and anticipation was already boiling in my gut. I had a lineup of interviews in Nashville over the next two days, and all of them were scheduled around one central meeting I had the next morning: an interview with Dave Ramsey.

As a boy growing up on the road with my dad, I had found myself constantly forced to listen to audiobooks and podcasts from leadership gurus that Dad would play through the car speakers. One of those people had frequently been Dave Ramsey, the Christian financial expert, radio personality, and bestselling author. When I was a kid, I hadn't known any of that stuff about Dave—just that he'd been fun to listen to while watching telephone poles flash by my window.

But as I grew older, I began to look up to Dave more and more until eventually his passion and wisdom as a Christ-following entrepreneurial leader made him a hero to me.

That's why, as I now made my way toward Nashville, heavy anticipation was already setting in. Nervousness and doubly intense excitement clashed inside me. With tremendous help from Dave's team as well as from some other people who had helped vouch for me, I had finally earned thirty minutes face to face with Dave and had intentionally flexed my schedule to make him the 250th interview in my project as a way of memorializing the event. Now, I was just hours away from showtime.

My dad and brother Heston were tagging along with me for the fun of the trip, Dad in the passenger's seat and Heston in the back. When I finally arrived in Nashville that evening, we all decided to drive straight to downtown and explore the city together. Growing up in the Midwest, I've learned to enjoy country music, and Nashville sure had plenty of it!

The first place we visited was a bar on a street corner with every door swung wide to showcase the live band playing inside: a drummer in the back, guitarists and singers in front, and a violinist who pranced along the top of the bar counter as she made her violin sing. After Heston and I had our fill of root beer, we went on to check out the rest of the city. By nightfall, we were having such a good time we could hardly stand to go to our hotel and fall asleep!

The next morning, we got ready, enjoyed breakfast at a nearby café, and headed over to the headquarters of Ramsey Solutions. Once we got there, we momentarily hung out in Martha's Place, a coffee shop adjoined to the lobby of the building. Then we were escorted backstage, behind the recording studio, to a boardroom. Dave Ramsey walked in right after us and greeted us with, "Hello, gentlemen! How are y'all doing today?"

I beamed a grin and said, "Hey Mr. Ramsey! I'm Holden. And I'm doing better than I deserve!"

At that, he grinned back—I'd just used one of his own personal phrases.

Against the Current

A thousand questions surged through my mind like currents in the sea as Dave and I started our conversation, but one of those questions in particular held my attention at a focal point. It was the prime question I had come anxious to ask, and while I've scattered Dave's responses to various questions throughout this book, his response to this particular question was the most personally impactful quote I got from him. My question was, "Mr. Ramsey, why is it that you continue to lead even when it would seem so much easier and safer to follow?"

After a thoughtful twenty seconds, Dave said, "Holden, it's not easier and safer to follow like people may assume. The only way it's easier and safer to follow is to be under the illusion that the leader knows what they're doing.

"It's like a paycheck. I can count on a steady paycheck, but someone's got to put the money in the bank to cause that payroll to clear, so it's not safer. That's an illusion. And it's not easier because, when you're leading, you actually get to make up the rules.

"But the reason to lead, now that I've been doing it twenty-five years, is the tremendous satisfaction in your soul—the quality of people you get to hang out with and quality of work that gets created when you lead well. It's enough of a reason to lead just to do that. It's amazing."

I was left dumbfounded by Mr. Ramsey's response, not because I disagreed with it or found it repulsive, but because I found it fascinating. I'd never heard anything like it. *"Following isn't safer or easier, that's an illusion..."* I repeated in my head.

After our conversation concluded—not thirty minutes later like the plan had been, but an *hour* later thanks to Dave's permission to extend our time—I sat in the lobby of Ramsey Solutions with my dad and brother to watch Dave in the recording studio for a live broadcast. My mind raced with questions and thoughts, and I found myself recalling moments in my own past when I had chosen to follow rather than lead. These weren't times I'd simply ranked lower than someone else in terms of authority; no, these were times that I'd *thought* like a follower.

I recalled time's I had jeered at and belittled someone simply to fit in with everyone else around me who did the same, even though I silently burned with anger and a desire to stand up for them.

Times I'd taken flirting too far, taking advantage of the attention I received from girls to feed my own emotional voids, though I was disgusted with myself the entire time.

Times I'd used words to trash good friends of mine behind their backs simply to "impress" the people I was currently with.

Those memories came and went in the span of a second, and a hundred others just like them followed.

Then a question entered my mind: *"The crowd runs from risk and difficulty, so isn't following the crowd safer and easier?"*

It only took me a moment before I answered myself. *"No."* The word echoed in my head, disbanding any other doubts I'd had before mentally saying it. In my brief moment of soul-searching, something had become blatantly obvious to me: every time I followed the safe and easy path, ironically, it made me feel scared to death and weak as a toothpick.

Since then, the truth I've come to find is that following everyone else in life—I mean, going along with what everyone else does, following everyone else to where they're going, and trying to be like everyone else—feels safe and easy for a little bit. In fact, as far as dying or being harmed, following is about as safe as you can get so long as you don't try to break the mold.

But that's the deadly part. The lethality of following isn't that it kills you, but rather that it merely keeps you from ever truly coming alive in the first place. If you choose to spend your life clinging to the security you find in the world and conforming yourself to fit in, it will work. You can probably make it through life and die without hardly a scratch on you, but it will come at a cost.

Like Justin Mecklenburg, a Christ-driven entrepreneur from Kingfisher, Oklahoma, told me, "One of the worst things a leader can do is go stagnate. If you aren't growing, then you're dying." The same way ponds dry up and go stagnant when they have no inflow of water, so we also go stale and rancid when we cling to where we are. The security of the world and the call of your heart lead two different directions, and following one will sacrifice the other. So here's the basic question:

Would you rather hide in the security of the world and die with rot in your heart, or chase the call of your heart and die with scars on your skin?

It's often easy to let uncertainty hold us back from trying something. However, throughout my own experiences, I've learned that life is a lot like rock climbing: to chase the adventure God calls you toward, you have to tear your hands off of what makes you feel secure and comfortable, and by risk and grit, climb.

As Bobby Gruenewald, innovator of the YouVersion Bible app which has over 300 million downloads, told me, "We make the mistake of planning our future based on what we can do now. Rather, we should plan for a future that demands our growth, because if your vision is smaller than your potential, you won't move."

To chase the adventure God calls you on, you have to stop protecting who you've always been and go discover who you're made to be. Stop letting the current of everyone else drag you, and dare to lead against the current. Like Mat Staver, a lawyer and the founder of the litigation non-profit Liberty Counsel, said to me, "If there's peace in your heart, follow it even if there are questions in your mind."

Fight the Current

Who are you? Do you even know? I didn't used to know, and I still don't know fully. Every single day I fight the temptation of fear to chase what feels safe, to mutilate who I am, to bow my backbone of conviction and smother my heart of passion in exchange for the feeling of security. But what I know is that we'll never discover who we're made to be by succumbing to who everyone else tells us to be.

We all want to change the world, thinking we could make things better, truer, and more full of life. Deeper than our desires for safety and comfort, we long to be the pioneer. We want to live a life that matters. But maybe you're like me and you've wondered, *"What could I ever do that matters? I'm just one person."* It's a fair question. But the truth is that one person can change the entire world.

US Senator James Lankford of Oklahoma once told me, "Impact starts with one person." That's all it takes. One person. You. Because when you are willing to fight for what's right even when everyone else thinks the fight is futile, suddenly, someone will stand and join you. And then someone else. And then ten more. And then a thousand more. And then a million people will be fighting alongside *you*, the leader, not because you are in charge, but because you dare to move against the current.

Mark Floyd, the CFO of Ramsey Solutions (Dave Ramsey's company) explained to me, "If you're coasting, that means you're flowing with the current. And whenever you're flowing with the current, that means you're going the wrong direction." What we often fail to acknowledge is that before we can ever change anything, we first have to stay true to ourselves.

To make an impact on the world, you have to *lead*, and the person you have to lead is you. Because in the end, the only ones who ever leave their mark on the world are the ones who dare to be different than it—people who choose to follow the God-given call of their heart and fight for what's right even if doing so means veering off the road well traveled and venturing into the storm.

To make a difference, you have to be different. You have to fight the current and break the mold. That's the first step. Because, remember, only those who dare to be different than the world will ever change it, and unless you lead yourself to become who you are made to be, you'll end up conforming yourself to everyone else.

So, who are you? When the illusion of safety and the call of God split ways like a fork in a river, who are you? Are you a member of the crowd who plays it safe and goes with the flow? Or are you the pioneer who is willing to venture off the road well traveled, fight the current of the world, and lead the way to where God calls you?

Chapter 5

MIND OF A BEAST

"You will never find yourself by protecting yourself."
—Dr. Lew Sterrett,
speaker, horse trainer, interview #4

"Come on dude! Give me something to work with!"

"Let's see what you can do!"

"Kick some dirt up!"

My friends' voices shot down the road to me as I turned my four-wheeler around and faced them again. They were all situated around a bend in a road, GoPro cameras ready as they anticipated my next "drift"—a driving maneuver in which the driver throws the momentum of the car, or in my case, the four-wheeler, and causes the vehicle to slide sideways around the bend or corner of a road.

At only a couple months into my interviews project in October of 2014, I was still the insecure hotshot who had just quit basketball and now "traveled the country and interviewed celebrities"—at least, that's what my attitude said. My friends and I were shooting a short action video during the annual father-son camping trip that the men and boys in our circle of friends have at our family's ranch.

On this occasion, I had already successfully completed a dozen or so drifts around the bend. I knew from past experience that the stunt normally makes for a pretty cool camera-shot due to all the loose gravel and dirt that the four-wheeler kicks up and sprays everywhere as it slides sideways.

But now, after half an hour of my friends and I driving over this particular spot, it was starting to become bare. We'd accidentally kicked almost all of the gravel off the road and into the grass by having driven over it so many times. As a result, I could no longer kick up the spectacular display of dirt and rocks that I had been able to showcase previously. That is, unless I increased my velocity.

With all my friends camera-ready, and knowing that this particular camera-shot could make me look like a rock star, I narrowed my gaze. The adventure and excitement of activities like this were usually enough to draw me to them naturally, but in this moment, my normal motivation for adventure became replaced with a ravenous hunger for glory.

I found myself in a spell of addiction to my image, mindless of the consequences like a substance addict suddenly afflicted with desire. I knew drifting the corner at any speed or intensity higher than that which I'd already exhibited was beyond my skill range, but something in me snapped and madness seized my mind. I gunned the gas.

I approached the turn in full throttle and with gaze focused, the gravelly roar of the engine beneath me drowning out the excited whoops and hollers of my friends. At the last second, I planted my feet into the footholds, threw my body sideways against the momentum of the four-wheeler, whipped the steering bar sideways as far as the axle would allow, and used my body weight to throw the back end of my four-wheeler perpendicular to the road.

I nailed it—or, at least I thought I did for just a moment. After rounding the corner sideways against the road with the right side of my four-wheeler in front, I felt a dreadful jerk as both my right-side tires hit a deep layer of gravel and caught a little too much traction. As a result, my body weight leaning off the far left side of my four-wheeler suddenly proved insufficient to counterbalance the force trying to flip it.

In a split second, the four-wheeler rolled and slammed me against the gravel road at at least thirty miles an hour, sending me sprawling. The four-wheeler didn't stop, either. We both tumbled down the road with me saying a prayer for each time that the four-wheeler crashed, flew in the air above me, and crashed again, that it didn't land on top of me. The crash ended just as fast as it had started, and I hurriedly scrambled to my feet.

Only then did I notice and feel the gashes covering my body, most noticeably the fact that the palms of my hands didn't have skin on them. It wasn't until after my friends had rushed to help me stumble to the house, wash the gravel out of my flesh, and wrap my hands in gauze that I noticed both of my arms, my right shoulder, and the entire right half of my back were also skin bare.

But somehow, through all the pain, something felt good: I had attracted the attention of all my friends there at the camping trip, and they were all star-struck impressed with me.

And that gave me a sickening pleasure.

Letting Go

Leading into my project of interviews and over the next year or so afterward, I found most of my confidence and self-worth in an image I'd built for myself as being a wild and crazy daredevil. I was addicted to it.

I believe it's one thing for a boy to be wild, adventurous, overly confident, and want to impress his friends; that's something I applaud and encourage. But that wasn't my problem. My daredevil feats weren't performed out of confidence, but rather, a lack of it—and *that* was my problem.

My sense of identity came from people being impressed with me. All my friends knew me as a reckless thrill-seeker willing to take on any dare, and I was proud to flaunt it. But as I look back, I know that the reason I pushed myself so hard to appear "scared of nothing" was because deep inside, I was scared to death of being rejected by people. And because, beneath my daredevil persona, I thought it was my only way of getting people to like and respect me.

However, that wasn't the real me. I mean, I was definitely a risk taker at heart, but somehow, it just felt fake being "fearless" when the reason for it was to hide from what I was truly afraid of. I wasn't fearless. If anything, I was reckless, and deep down, that disgusted me.

But as I continued on my journey of interviews, I started noticing how certain people would often speak openly about their weaknesses and struggles. Even the biggest and baddest people of all didn't flaunt their success and power, but on the contrary, were often the humblest and most vulnerable. While I used what accomplishments and glory I had to hide my insecurity, these people didn't. It was almost as if by living in openness about their own weaknesses, struggles, pain, fear, and insecurity, it made them stronger.

Eventually, I got to where I craved what I saw in these people. While I was held captive by fear to my image, these people were free. And eventually, my own desperate longing to be free gave me the courage to attempt what I saw these people had done: let go.

As Lew Sterrett, my horse-breaking friend and mentor would later reinforce to me, "You have to let go of who you appear to be to discover who you might be."

Letting go of who I appeared to be in order to discover who I was meant to be required a different kind of risk than I was used to. No easily healed broken bones, scraped skin, or bruises. This risk was exposing my heart. It was dropping the facades I'd held up so long and letting who I was underneath become what everyone else saw.

I didn't go around putting my true colors on display for everyone to see. How other people saw me was no longer the point. For me, the change was subtle, and at first, I doubt anyone noticed. Honestly, people probably see me as daredevil now more so than ever, because my true colors are that of a Christ-driven adventurer. But *I* noticed, and that's what matters—because though letting go of the mask you hide behind will eventually change the way others see you, the point of it is changing the way you see yourself.

I've found that as long as you are chasing acceptance and security, you will never fully become who you are made to be. Finding acceptance and security means compromising who you are at the core, as well as gathering "stuff"—material, success, control—around yourself. The thing is, though, the stuff you gather in life can blow away with the wind.

The only thing that truly stands permanent is the man or woman you chisel yourself into. That's why, as my father has taught me, to be true to yourself and grow into the person you were born to become, you have to focus more on who you're becoming than on what you're getting.

Stephan Moore, leader of a camp for inner city kids in Oklahoma called Shiloh, once told me, "Don't choose things for what they will do for you, but for what they will make of you." If you try to find purpose after already obtaining acceptance, you won't be able to, because you'll be held back by the image you constantly have to maintain.

However, if you chase purpose first, if you chase the call God has placed on your heart first, and stand up for what you believe in first, then you won't need acceptance since you are no longer trying to fit in—rather, you're now leading. You can chase acceptance by fitting in with everyone else, or fulfillment by following your own heart, but you cannot chase both.

If you choose to chase your heart and stand for what's right, it will cost you acceptance and security. What's right isn't often popular. And all the world asks for in return for acceptance and security is that you tame your heart of passion, and bow your backbone of conviction. Then you can be popular, accepted, and surrounded by a cheering crowd.

But from personal experience, I know following your heart is far better. Why? Because everyone else will start to realize who you really are. There will be people who begin to rise up alongside you, and people who begin to rise up against you, but I'll tell you what—having a family of like-minded leaders alongside you, even at the cost of having enemies who stand against you, is far better than having neither.

Besides, the confidence that comes from everyone else's approval of you when you're simply creating an image for yourself is fake confidence. It's not confidence in who you are, but in who people tell you that you are. And here's the problem with that: When you place your worth in someone else's hands, you constantly have to go back to them for it.

That's why true confidence can never be found in others opinions, no matter how good or bad those opinions may be. It's like something Tripp Crosby of the comedy duo "Tripp and Tyler" told me about himself: "When I started getting thrown in front of audiences and getting applause, I got a jolt of confidence, but it wasn't good. True confidence comes from inside you, not outside."

Everyone else is going to constantly tell you who you should be. Because it feels comfortable to simply accept that, that's what you'll be tempted to do—but don't. Becoming who you're made to be starts with letting go of the identity everyone else throws on you and pushing yourself toward who God made you to be.

This is what I've come to know as being a "beast"—abandoning the ease and fantasized security of the wandering flock, and instead daring to follow the Shepherd whose call is "Take up your cross daily, and follow me."

How to Eat Steak

It was December of 2015, and I was on the road to Houston, Texas, to meet two people Dave Ramsey had suggested I interview: David and Jason Benham, also known as the Benham brothers.

Identical twins, these brothers had both been professional baseball players in the minor leagues and had gone on to become successful entrepreneurs, speakers, and authors. They had starred in and produced a home-remodeling show called *Flip It Forward* on HGTV a few years ago and made headlines when the network canceled the show after the brothers had refused to compromise their biblical views on abortion and homosexuality.

Since then, they've continued to write and speak, thrive as entrepreneurs, and train other leaders. From what I knew about them, I admired their passion, drive, and willingness to take a stand for what they believed in, and by my best guess, I was betting that these guys knew what it meant to be a beast. I was right.

The Benham brothers lived in North Carolina, and though I often did travel out of state for interviews, it was beyond my budget to travel all the way to North Carolina just to meet with the two of them. I could have easily asked for a conversation with them over the phone, but something in me wanted more. Something I'd learned by then was that getting to know the people I interviewed was even more valuable than what I could learn from them, and I always connected with people better in person.

While it would have been just fine for me to talk with David and Jason over the phone, as long as I could find a way to make it work for me to meet them in person, I wasn't down with "just fine." So when I reached out to the brothers, I stressed that I wanted to meet with them in person if at all possible and was willing to drive to any neighboring state of Oklahoma if by chance they would be traveling west.

As it turned out, they were on a speaking tour and would be in Houston, Texas, the following week, which other than one interview I would need to reschedule, worked great for me. Four days later, I was bound for Houston.

It's not always possible to go as far as I did that time to live out adventure, but whenever it's not possible to go that far, you won't need to. What I've found is that adventure and awesome are always just a little bit farther away than fine and normal, and they're always achievable if you'll just push yourself a bit more. Sometimes, a phone call *is* an adventure, depending on what it took to get the phone call. It's like my dad has taught me: The difference between ordinary and extraordinary is *extra*.

It was an eight-hour drive, so I spent the time listening to audiobooks by Bill Hybels and Jefferson Bethke. When I finally got to Houston, the highways become so enormous that I could have sworn some of them had twenty lanes. Eventually arriving at the venue where the Benham brothers were speaking, I called their assistant, Suzi, to let her know I was there. Then I waited in the lobby of the adjoining hotel to hear back from the brothers.

"Hey, Holden! This is David!" said the voice on my phone a few minutes later.

"Hey, David! Good to be talking with you!"

"You, too. Suzi told me you're here. Jason and I are in our hotel room and can come downstairs in a minute. Do you want to talk with us together or separate?"

I really hadn't thought much about that. However, since I usually did my interviews one on one, I responded, "I'll just talk with you guys separately if that works!"

Five minutes later, David walked out of the elevator. He and I began chatting, but something nagged at me from the back of my mind. Finally, I realized it was his earlier question about whether to talk with him and Jason separately or together. Did they know something I didn't know?

So I asked David, "I really want to learn from you and your brother. I hadn't really considered whether I should talk with you and Jason separately or together when you asked me that on the phone, so let me ask you: would I learn more from talking with you guys separately or together?"

David smiled and said, "Together! We really feed off of each other."

"Well, would you call him and get him down here then?" I asked excitedly and with a sarcastic grin. David grinned back and took his phone out of his pocket.

An hour later, David, Jason, and I had migrated to the hotel cafe, where the two brothers insisted on buying me a steak. They'd each had a steak at the same restaurant previously that day, now claiming that they might have been some of the best steaks they'd ever eaten—but there was no need to sell me on it. Behind my smile and contented appearance, I was starving and probably would have eaten orange peels if they'd been offered.

When my steak finally came out, it smelled delicious. I would describe it in more detail, but honestly, I was so hungry that all appreciations for the meal other than *"This is steak"* eluded me. Feeling I was in the presence of two strapping men, I forfeited my manners and tore into the steak with my knife and fork like a Viking.

After a couple of bites, I realized David and Jason were both watching me. Jason smiled and shook his head, then interrupted my meal by saying, "Holden, you're embarrassing to watch!" He laughed. "Let me show you how to cut a steak."

A little ashamed of my eating, I watched as he cut firmly and precisely, instructing me on manners that seemed overly-sophisticated as he did so. In that moment, I realized that my mother had actually been right with her incessant dinnertime lectures on eating etiquette. No matter who I was with, it would always be wise to remember that polite manners and courteous behavior were not signs of being prissy, but rather of respect.

Ten minutes later, our interview was coming to a close since David and Jason both needed to return to their room soon and finish getting ready for the event that night. With a slanted smirk, I asked my last question.

"I'm just one among hundreds of people who have interviewed you guys. Y'all have been asked more questions than I'd dare to imagine. So let me ask this: What's a question that no one's asking you guys that you wish they were?"

David and Jason raised their eyebrows at each other, taken by pleasant surprise. They discussed between themselves for a moment, shutting each other down on a few question ideas, and then came to an agreement when David suggested, "Why were we willing to lose it all?"

I knew what David meant. By standing for their faith, they'd lost their TV show. They'd lost their old reputation and fame. They'd lost countless business opportunities. And that was just the tip of the iceberg because really, I had no idea the abyss of sacrifice that lay beneath the surface. After writing the question down in my journal, I then flipped it on them, asking, "Well then, why were you guys willing to lose it all?"

Without hesitation, they both answered, "Because we serve God's kingdom."

Made by Choices

I slept at my Aunt Beverly's and Uncle Harold's house in Houston that night. After eating breakfast with them the next morning, I turned my gaze toward home. On the long drive, I found myself thinking deeply about everything the Benham brothers and I had discussed the night before, especially the final comment they'd made to me about why they'd been willing to lose everything.

Most of us look at people like the Benham brothers and think that they have the strength to stand for something and risk losing everything because they're already amazing. That's what amazing leaders do, right? They stand for what's right even at the expense of losing everything they have, and they can do that because they're strong enough. But the rest of us could never do that, because we don't have the strength or influence of beasts like the Benham brothers, who reside at the head of the pack.

Or is that really how things work?

As the miles flew past on my drive home from Houston, something became clear to me. David and Jason's resolve to stand for what's right had existed long before they'd had roaring support from thousands of fans. Their strength to lead came from a resolve to follow Christ, not from a cheering crowd.

The truth is that beasts aren't beasts because they're leading at the head of the pack like we all think. They aren't beasts because they're the team captain, the national champion, or the best. Those are results of being a beast, but they're not the source.

Beasts are beasts because long before they were ever leading at the head of the pack, they had the mind of a beast in the back of the pack.

Beasts *think* like leaders. Not because they're in charge or because they're the most talented or because they've "made it" and want everyone to know it, but because a beast is who they choose to be: the best version of themselves.

They choose to take initiative for where they go instead of drifting with the current and following the crowd. They choose to take initiative to become who they're made to be instead of allowing time and chance to turn them into average and normal. They choose to seize life rather than let life suffocate and control them. They embrace the difficulty and love the challenge.

Like David Benham told me early on in our conversation, "The real leaders step into the pain cave and make a fire there and get used to it. Others step back and play it safe, taking the easy way and missing the opportunity to grow into more of who God made them to be."

To fully live out the adventure of who God made you to be, you also have to be ready to take on the battles of becoming that person. That is why passion is often short-lived without discipline, grit, and resolve. Without the resolute heart and steeled mentality earned through embracing the "pain cave," you'll back out before you make it through.

Beasts do what no one else wants to do and what has to be done even when nobody is watching because, in the end, they're not doing it because they're told to. Rather, it's because they know that to go where God calls them to go and to become who they're called to be, being their best is what's required. The cross we carry is the calling Christ gives us, and beasts carry the cross.

We are made by the choices we make every day, and beasts are made by one choice in particular: Will I take up my cross and follow the Shepherd, or run from the danger and difficulty my calling entails and follow the flock? It's up to you. Just remember that before you'll ever carry the strength, talent, and influence of a beast in your hands, you have to carry the resolve, determination, and conviction of a beast in your mind.

I dare you, look within yourself to define who you are and stop trying to please people or play a part for the approval of others. You can't please everyone and you weren't meant to. Instead, embrace the originality of who you are and live for an audience of One.

As Ralph Drollinger, the former NBA basketball player and now the founder of Capitol Ministries—a discipleship and evangelism ministry for top political leaders in the US—told me, "Some saints have rope burns on their back, and some saints have rope burns on their neck. The strength to take the whip lashes on your back or the courage to wear the hanging noose around your neck comes from having God as your final and only audience. Then you'll have the courage, tenacity, and motivation to do what's right."

Breaking the Cycle

It has been over three years since that day I flipped my four-wheeler and crashed. That day I pushed my limits to prove what a daredevil I was so that my friends would be impressed with me. That day I pushed my limits for the wrong reasons.

Flash forward a year, and what I was once faced with at sixteen-years-old I was faced with again, at seventeen. The setting was different, but the risk I faced was similar.

I was standing on a fifteen-foot rock ledge in Shark's Cove on the north shore of Oahu. On vacation there with my family, I had climbed to the highest point above the cove, where I stood looking down at the ocean and rolling swells beneath me, trying to persuade myself to do a backflip.

My sister, Brianna, was with me, and I had my waterproof GoPro camera strapped to my wrist. The first time we had climbed up to the ledge, I had dove off, used my GoPro to film Brianna doing a front flip, and then climbed back up, this time excited to capture a backflip on video. I was only an amateur, but I still had my share of experience cliff jumping and had back-flipped off heights of twenty-five to thirty feet multiple times before. So, when I had climbed up the jagged rocks, I really hadn't even considered I might hesitate to make the jump.

I turned my back to the sea, calming myself before launching backward into a flip. Brianna was holding the GoPro ready to capture the shot, and dude, it was going to be a cool one. Squatting down, I tried to force myself to jump.

But I couldn't.

I was frozen.

Ten minutes went by as I tried to talk myself into jumping, and I still couldn't do it. Stalling for time, I got off the edge briefly and made the mistake of opening my GoPro case and trying to wipe a smudge off the camera lens with my damp board shorts. This caused the lens to fog over completely. There went my hope of getting a sweet picture, because it would take a few hours for the salty moisture to evaporate from the camera.

Tired of debating with myself, I was about to just dive into the water again and give up on doing the backflip—after all, I wasn't even going to get the shot.

But something stopped me. I turned my back to the ocean once again. In that moment, I knew the jump had just become about something much bigger than getting a cool picture for Instagram. If I were to let myself back out now, I would find it easier to back out of other situations in the future. If I allowed myself to run away now, I would be running away the rest of my life until I finally turned and faced the fear chasing me. I refused to run.

Standing on the ledge, I closed my eyes in self-reflection. The GoPro was out of service and there would be no cool picture of this. Instead, in a way I had seldom done before, I committed the jump to the glory of God. I figured if God continued to call me to be part of accomplishing incredible things, living out the adventure for which he had created me, and fighting on behalf of his kingdom, I would need to trust him completely.

In following Christ, I was going to need to be a lot braver and trust God a lot more than what it was going to take to do a backflip off a petty fifteen-foot ledge, so I might as well start now.

With my perspective shifted and knowing in my heart that this jump was about something bigger than me, a peace came over me. Somehow, I knew that if I was doing this for God, He would carry me through. As I reopened my eyes, fear's voice went silent. I squatted down, leaned back, and launched myself off the cliff.

For Whose Glory?

When I surfaced in the sun-basked water below, I laughed, let out a whoop-holler, and did a fist pump. I had nailed the flip perfectly. I know cliff diving isn't for everyone, and for some people trusting God might even mean *not* taking such a crazy physical risk. But for me, that jump meant the world because I knew why I had just done it—not to be a daredevil, not to get a crazy sweet shot to post online, and not to impress anyone.

I'd done it simply to be who God made me to be: for his glory and my joy.

Swimming back to shore with Brianna, I remembered something Chris Brown, part of Dave Ramsey's team and the host of the nationally syndicated radio show *True Stewardship,* had once told me: "The difference between risk and stupid is, do I feel called to do this? Am I doing it for my own glory or for God's?"

I definitely learned that lesson that day. There's a thin line that separates crazy from faith, and it has nothing to do with what you're doing; rather, the difference is in why you're doing it.

Looking back now, the jump itself wasn't even that big of a deal. It was just a fifteen-foot backflip, and I'd easily done backflips off points almost twice that height. But on the other hand, it was a *huge* deal. Rex Crain, my motivational speaker friend from California, once told me, "The problem when it comes to courage is acting on feeling. You are never what you feel; you are what you decide."

Having the mind of a beast means choosing who you will be when you're at the top of your own cliffs in life. You aren't what you feel in that moment looking down; you are who you decide to be. Everyone feels fear—especially the brave. Without fear, bravery wouldn't exist.

What separates the cowards from the brave isn't that one feels fear and the other doesn't, but that one lets fear break them and the other breaks fear. You don't get to decide if you're afraid, but you do get to decide if, in response to that fear, you're going to be a wuss or a warrior.

With every fear you face, you have the choice to either conquer or to run, and with every time you make that choice, you further define who you are. You can be a victim of your circumstances, of your family, of your limitations, and of your problems. Or you can decide to be a beast. You can run from your fears and remain imprisoned yet unscathed, or you can face your fears and bear the scars to prove it.

Flawless skin, or freedom. Which will it be?

Chapter 6

IN LOVE WITH THE JOURNEY

"Be authentic to who you are, and the opportunities to do whatever it is you're called to are going to be out there."

—Scott Hamilton,
Olympic gold medalist figure skater, interview #476

In late summer of 2015, at over halfway through my interviews, I was about to embark on a journey I'd wanted to take for a long time: an overnight road trip on my own, without parents or other adults. This was several months prior to my solo trip to Houston. At seventeen, I had traveled all over Oklahoma and even to Arkansas by myself as part of my interviews project, but I had never stayed overnight anywhere without Dad or another adult present—that is, not until now. I had a lineup of interviews in Branson, Missouri, over the course of two days, and had my mind set on making this trip solo.

It didn't take much on my part to get my parents on board with my idea. Two boys my family has always admired are the Abernathy brothers of Oklahoma. I grew up hearing stories from my grandmother of how Louis and Temple Abernathy set out in 1910 by horseback from Oklahoma to Santa Fe, and then on to New York City with the expectation of meeting President Roosevelt there upon his return from hunting in Africa.

Sure, cool enough—but what makes the story crazy is that they were no more than six and ten years old at the time and made the trip all by themselves!

In the end, even though I wanted to go without my parents, I did talk to my younger brother Heston about joining me for the trip, and he was all in. Branson is about a five-hour drive from our house, so the two of us headed out at 7 a.m. in the morning with the audiobook version of *Love Works* by Joel Manby playing on the AUX to keep us company.

With our windows down and hair blowing wildly in the wind, the miles passed quickly. Once we got about an hour away from Branson, I had Heston look up a couple hotels in the area to see if any of them had rooms.

Whenever my dad and I went on road trips together, Dad would often just pop in at any random hotel when we got tired and reserve a room on the spot. So, as far as I was concerned, I was really being proactive by calling ahead that morning. We called the first hotel that came up as listed in Branson but found out they didn't rent rooms to fifteen- and seventeen-year-olds. Neither did the next hotel we called. And neither did the next one. Come to find out, not renting rooms to minors was a thing.

I didn't panic. I remembered that my first appointment in Branson that afternoon was with Adam Donyes, the founder of Link Year, an organization that provides biblical leadership training for young adults and works closely with Kanakuk Kamps, the Christian youth and family camp organization I talked about in Chapter 1.

Joe White, the CEO of Kanakuk Kamps in Branson, was the one who had actually suggested I talk with Adam in the first place, so I decided to email Joe and ask if he knew of any place Heston and I could stay the night. Worst-case scenario, I figured we could sleep in our car. But neither one of us were fond of that idea, so we were definitely not giving up on figuring out another option.

As of then, however, I had no idea what the alternative could possibly be.

Grateful

We arrived at Kanakuk, which was where Link Year would be taking place in a few months, and I spent an hour talking with Adam Donyes.

With every word Adam spoke, his passion for discipling and raising up young warriors of God's kingdom became more and more evident. One of the things he told me was, "Wisdom is gained through life lived, God's word, and other people. To gain wisdom, don't talk about it, *be* about it."

After wrapping up with Adam, I caught up with some of the other staff and employees I knew from years past at Kanakuk. Pretty soon, it was time for my next appointment—an interview with Jack Herschend, the co-founder and former CEO of the Silver Dollar City Corporation. Silver Dollar City is an 1880s Americana-style theme park located in the heart of the Ozark Mountains in Branson. I grew up visiting there every year or two with my family, and with its wild roller coasters and rugged style, it was my boyhood paradise.

Exploring the park as a boy, I would occasionally wonder about the leader of Silver Dollar City and imagine what he or she looked like. I knew nothing about Jack Herschend, only that someone in his role must exist. Finally meeting him, I was ecstatic. I approached him with hand extended and an uncontrollably excited smile, thinking, "No way! I'm shaking the hand right now of that mysterious legend I used to imagine!"

My interview with Mr. Herschend was incredible, and he told me something that day I've remembered ever since: "My very best days are the days I think the least about myself. If my day ends with a pity party, it wasn't much of one." Since then, I've come to learn the truth in Mr. Herschend's words.

Some people would claim that the wealthiest people in the world are also the most miserable. I don't believe that's strictly true. It *can* be true, but it can also be just as true with completely broke people. Joy isn't bought. Passion isn't bought. Adventure isn't bought.

Being rich doesn't make people miserable. Rather, believing

you can acquire enough stuff to make life worthwhile is what makes people miserable. As one of my best friend's dad, Mr. Farris, who is like another father to me, once told me, "To appreciate the things to come, you have to be grateful for what you have now."

After meeting with Mr. Herschend, Heston and I stopped at a gas station to fuel up our pickup truck and grab a drink. Then I got a phone call.

"This is Holden," I answered.

"Hi Holden! This is Amy, Joe White's assistant. Joe had told me that you and your brother are looking for somewhere to spend the night tonight, and asked me to find out if we had a cabin here at Kanakuk that could accommodate you both. As it turns out, we do! If you and your brother want, you're welcome to sleep here at K-1 tonight."

Unable to contain my excitement, my jaw dropped in an open-mouth smile. I blurted, "Yes! That would be awesome!" into my phone, gave an ecstatic thank you, and ended the call after gathering the essential details from Amy. K-1 was one of Kanakuk's camps—in fact, the first summer camp Heston and I had ever attended as boys.

As soon as Heston came walking out of the gas station holding two Gatorades in his hands, I announced the news to him. By this point, we had decided that if we didn't end up finding anywhere better to sleep, we would just go buy a cheap tent and two sleeping bags from Walmart and camp on the shore of Lake Taneycomo. However, we both agreed staying at Kanakuk was ten times cooler.

In high spirits, we headed back to Kanakuk and parked in front of K-1, and Amy showed us the cabin we would stay in. It was basic—one queen-sized bed for us to share and a bathroom—but as far as we were concerned, it might as well have been a palace. The fact that Kanakuk would let us stay with them, despite the fact that they gained *nothing* from it, made us more grateful for this single-bed cabin than we could have been for a five-star resort suite.

And that's what made the place so awesome to us—not what we were able to get, but the gratefulness we had.

As Far as You Can See

After moving our luggage into the cabin—which consisted of no more than Heston and I's backpacks—we had an hour before I was to meet with Garrett Perkins, one of the camp leaders that my friend Adam Martin had told me I should interview. Tired from our journey, Heston crashed for a nap.

I was about to change clothes and take a quick nap myself when I noticed Joe White—the camp's CEO and the man who had authorized our stay—walking down to our cabin with a bow and quiver.

Once he got close to our front door, he notched an arrow and released it at a target set up down the alleyway beside our cabin. I was tired, but I've always valued the chance to talk and hang out with someone as awesome as Mr. White. Plus, I had some intense gratitude to show in response to him letting us stay at Kanakuk, so I walked out of our cabin and greeted Mr. White. We talked for a good half hour as he shot and retrieved arrows.

I remember being inspired as I watched an older man in his late sixties tense his aged but bulging muscles, focus his gaze, and embed arrows deep into the center of his target. Why was he there? I mean, here at Kanakuk as the CEO, talking with and investing in some teenage kid, and working on his archery skills? Why was he still *pushing* himself?

As a successful older man, he could be kicked back on the patio of a beach bungalow somewhere, retired and enjoying life. That's what most people would be doing, so why wasn't he? I wanted to know.

Eventually, Mr. White wrapped up his target practice, and that evening after my last meeting, Heston and I headed to the Branson Landing to grab something to eat at Famous Dave's, one of our favorite BBQ restaurants. It was then that I found myself reflecting on the day and everything I'd learned.

I didn't have to be here. I mean, I didn't have to be here in Branson. A year ago, back at the start of my project, my initial agreement with my dad was that I got a vehicle after completing the 500 interviews.

However, our deal had said nothing about me having to do interviews with people from other states.

But whatever. So I managed to land some interviews with people from out of state, but who said I actually had to go see them? I could have stayed home, completed my interviews with a couple hours on the phone, and been done with it. It definitely would have been easier. But I hadn't.

And then there was Heston. Heston had decided to miss out on a party and several other activities back home, do extra school work in advance, and take two days out of his week to accompany me on a trip that really had no direct or immediate benefits for him. It would have been perfectly fine for him to stay home, but he hadn't.

And in the end, we now found ourselves chilling on the lakefront patio outside Famous Dave's—eating some of the best barbecue ever, watching the night lights dance on the rippling surface of Lake Taneycomo, and breathing memories of an unforgettable trip into our consciousness like the fresh air we breathed into our lungs. It was awesome, and it was worth a thousand times the ease and convenience we would have saved by settling for "fine."

It was while sitting there on that patio that I realized the adventure of life is found by pushing the boundaries and exploring the frontier, not by settling where you are. I've found that in life, "fine" will always come as a default. But if you want awesome, you'll have to step out of your comfort zone and *make* it awesome.

In the end, living without regrets isn't about getting everything you want and doing fine. Instead, it's about seeing as much and going as far as you possibly can. And to do that, you're going to have to admit you have a long way to go.

Living without regrets isn't about maintaining your pride. It's about taking risks even though you may fail, daring to love even though you may not be loved back, and giving life everything you've got despite what you may not get in return.

Be *you*, give life everything you've got, and let nothing hold you back. Not the fear of messing up, because messing up is how you'll become better. Not the pursuit of safety, because safety is not what you were made for. Not the opinions of others, because you were born to be you. From what I've learned, the rule of "no regrets" means you go as far as you can see—and when you get there, you'll always be able to see farther.

Windows Down

"Dad, come on!" I exclaimed. "It looks the same as Oklahoma City!"

I was eleven years old, and Dad and I were on a business road trip making our way through Tennessee, toward Memphis. For the past few hours I'd been free to keep to myself, listen to music, and read. However, now that Memphis was in view on the horizon, Dad was insisting that I start looking outside. I'd been fighting him on the issue for a couple minutes, until he'd finally had enough.

"Put your earbuds and book away before I have to take them from you!" my dad said, raising his voice at me, and I grudgingly obeyed.

"Have you ever seen this part of the country?" Dad asked, knowing full well that I hadn't.

"No…" I murmured.

"So, when you get home and all your friends ask you what Memphis looked like, what are you gonna tell them? 'Uh, I don't know, I didn't bother looking?'" Dad paused for a moment, then said, "Listen, you need to learn to enjoy the journey. Look outside!"

This was typical. Every time I was in the car with Dad, or my family and I were on a big road trip, my mom and dad would make my siblings and me look outside, interact with each other, and be interested in the trip. It all had something to do with "enjoying the journey," as my dad called it.

Now approaching Memphis, I rolled my window down and stuck my arm outside, entertained by the feeling of air gushing around my open hand and parted fingers. As much as I resented being forced to refocus my attention away from the novel I was reading and toward the dancing light show in the distance—Memphis—I did like the feeling of wind in my face. And with the last pink glows of sunlight just barely visible on the edge of the horizon, I had to admit the sight of the city sure was spectacular. My dazzled fascination only increased as we drew closer.

Eventually, we were there, and I was in awe. That night, Dad and I found ourselves somewhere cool to eat and explored the city, which in the end left me reeling with excitement.

I've lived a hundred experiences just like that. Business trips with my dad and brothers to Iowa to make sale pitches. An evening spent cleaning house or cooking dinner with mom. A community project. A weekend spent working at our family ranch. Whatever it was, my parents always taught my siblings and me how to find adventure in otherwise boring and tedious activities—whether it was by exploring town, finding a new and awesome place to eat, meeting interesting people, talking with each other, taking the opportunity to learn something, or maintaining a quick wit for jokes.

As a result, I've finally come to learn that while adventure does exist in the grand and spectacular moments of life, it's something you'll also find just as much in the ordinary aspects of life.

You'll find it in the daily grind when you come to see work as an opportunity to create memories and laughter.

You'll find it in challenges when you view them as opportunities to test your limits and inspire others.

You'll find it when driving to town when you see the trip as an opportunity to connect with a friend, enjoy the wind, watch a sunset, feel the touch of rain, or enjoy the warm glow of sunlight on your skin.

As a matter of fact, if you don't find the adventure contained in the ordinary, the adventure of grander things will grow dull. It's like something Bob Goff, author of *Love Does*, told me when we first talked. I asked him how he continues to have such a zeal for life, and he said, "People lose their imagination and then they look old. I just stay curious."

If you don't maintain curiosity and imagination even in the

small and ordinary things, the vibrancy of the big things will die. You have to fall in love with the journey of life and the beauty of all that surrounds you or you'll get to the end of life only to realize fulfillment never existed in the glory, possessions, and awards you've accumulated—it existed along the journey of life, in every adventure you failed to enjoy.

You've got to fall in love with going somewhere, because if you just depend on getting somewhere to fulfill you, it never will.

Everyone is chasing something, but ultimately the ones who will find the chase most worthwhile are the ones who discover the adventure along the way, and whether you discover that adventure is up to you. If you want to find the adventure of life, I suggest looking outside. I dare you: try breathing the fresh wind, feeling the sunshine, and rolling the windows down.

Till I Die

Ever since the beginning of my interviews project, one man I'd always wanted to interview was John Maxwell, the leadership guru, author, and international speaker. As it turned out, near interview mark 300 in October of 2015, I got my wish.

I'd been in Atlanta, Georgia for the past week doing interviews and attending the Catalyst Conference, which is where I'd met Andy Mineo and Andy Stanley. It was at that time I got an invitation from the president of John Maxwell's company—David Hoyt, whom I'd interviewed earlier that week—to come hang out at a speaking event John was leading. David and I's secret hope was that I'd be able to snag a few minutes with John backstage during a break, but we wouldn't know until later on in the event if there would exist such an opportunity. In the meantime, that left me listening to John from out in the auditorium, taking notes, and enjoying the experience.

One thing John joked about during his first session was his age, sharing a question someone had asked him recently: "Are you going to die soon?" John's answer had been, "Well, I'm certainly not planning on it!" Everyone, including me, had a good laugh as he continued with the story.

But I saw more meaning in the story than just humor. John was roughly seventy years old, famous, and by my imagination, he was most certainly capable of a phenomenal retirement by now. Yet here he was, on stage in front of thousands of people, promoting his recent book and pushing himself.

John continued talking, having turned from jokes to the truth behind them that I'd already started to recognize. "I'm more passionate now than ever before, and I don't want to die any less passionate. I'm going to keep going harder and more passionate until I die."

"That sounds familiar," I thought to myself. Then I made the connection. It's what I'd picked up on while hanging out with Joe White a month earlier. Joe hadn't said it as plainly as John, but his actions had spoken for him. Both John and Joe pushed themselves relentlessly, like legendary athletes who had staked their claim in the hall of fame decades ago but *still* pushed themselves every day like they were training for a world title.

Despite my hopes of finding a time for John and I to talk, by the end of the event it was apparent that John simply wasn't going to have the space in his crazy schedule. However, John was having a private book signing later, and my point man, David Hoyt, suggested I might be able to chat with John there for a few minutes. That was enough for me—heck, I wasn't even supposed to be here!

When I finally got to see John at the book signing, I told him my name and what I was doing. I didn't figure he'd know who I was, but I was wrong. John beamed a smile and, with excitement, said he'd been hoping to meet me after having heard about me from some of his team during dinner the previous night. I immediately knew the members of his team he was talking about: Jason Grant, his company's global leadership developer; Chris Goede, his company's VP; and David Hoyt, his company's president, who had invited me to the event—all men I'd interviewed over the past few days.

Given the opportunity, I asked him, "Mr. Maxwell, what one thing, if nothing else, do you want the next generation of kingdom leaders to remember from you?"

He thought for a moment and then said, "This is what I'd tell your generation: learn all you can from the previous generation, and then build on top of it."

Funny, that's exactly what I was doing: learning all I could from those older and wiser than me. But the second part of John's statement, about "building on top of," stuck out to me more than the first part. Even after leaving John's event, the statement still haunted me.

"Build on top of it? Yeah, for a bit, but John you've built so high that you don't have to build any more! You've got everything you could ever want! So why are you still building?" I asked myself, mentally screaming the question into the blackness of my mind. I needed to know.

Most people just consume what they learn, using it to fill their own bellies and satisfy their own desires. I got that. I mean, pushing yourself to get what you want made sense. What didn't make sense was pushing yourself past that point.

Stay Hungry

"So, what did you learn?"

The question came from Dad and split the silence we'd been driving in for the past thirty minutes. It was several hours after we'd left John Maxwell's event, now nightfall, and we were on our way back toward home in Oklahoma—today had been our last day in Atlanta.

Sitting in the passenger seat, I took a deep breath and looked up through the windshield. I felt strangely irritable and agitated, devoid of my regular passion. Maybe answering this question would help.

But I couldn't remember learning anything that week. Oh sure, I'd *heard* lots of stuff and could have recited it, but that's not what Dad had asked. "Hmm," I said, "lots of stuff."

Dad rolled his eyes. "No way."

I bit my tongue and restrained a snide remark, surprised at my sudden attitude. I opened my mouth with the intent of having a more appropriate response, but my attitude swelled again and I shot back at Dad, "What, do you want me to get my journal out and read to you?"

Dad didn't retaliate, and just asked another calm question. "You've hit interview mark 300. What's your vision moving forward?"

I didn't know. For some reason, I'd totally lost it. My mind ran frantically, searching for where my sense of passion and purpose had disappeared to. I had just finished one of the most amazing trips of my journey, having talked with some of the most incredible people I could dream of meeting. I should have been brimming with passion right then, but instead, I felt empty.

"I. Don't. Know." I hissed, biting each word like a moody teenager and with eyes fixated on the dash.

Dad turned to look at me for a moment, then returned his vision to the road. "So, you're telling me we came all this way for a joyride, huh? Come on Holden, when people ask you what you learned from three days at Catalyst, from John Maxwell, from Andy Stanley, from a week trip to Atlanta, what are you going to tell them?"

That was it. I whipped my head around and yelled at Dad, "Didn't you hear me? I said I don't know!" That silenced the vehicle again, and I sat back in my seat and crossed my arms.

I'd been pushing myself like an animal recently, and for what? Well, to further the interview project. I was finally on a roll. I was finally closer to the end than I was to the beginning. I was pushing myself to get in touch with the greatest leaders I could. And why?

Once again, that question tore to my core: the reason I'd always dreamed of meeting John Maxwell was for how much I looked up to him, how much I was inspired by him, and how much I wanted to learn from him face to face. However, in the past week, my desire had slowly collapsed to simply wanting his famous, impressive, creditable name next to mine. What a small way to live.

I looked at Dad, a crack in my voice as I fought off tears, and whispered, "I don't know." With that, I grabbed my journal from my backpack and headlined a page. I journaled for the next hour by the dome light of the pickup, jotting down every self-indulgent desire for fame and success I could think of in an attempt to find something that would satisfy my deep-rooted yearning for… something. I didn't know what. It must be a desire for success. That's what it had always been in the past.

Over the next week, my thoughts turned to the answer John Maxwell had given me to my question: "Learn all you can from the previous generation, and then build on top of it."

"That's for you, right?" I would ask myself. The goal was to learn all you could, then build a mansion on top of it for yourself, right? Well, it hadn't been working for me. I sure as heck had been doing all I could to learn from the previous generation, but right then I felt stupider than a box of rocks. Getting what I wanted was supposed to fill me, but instead, it had left me starving.

The way I felt reminded me of a Bible verse I had never liked much: "Then I considered all that my hands had done and the toil I had expended in doing it, and behold, all was vanity and a striving after wind, and there was nothing to be gained under the sun" (Ecclesiastes 2:11).

I've always had a strong sense of ambition and drive, yet this verse in the Bible and others like it always used to confuse me because as far as I was concerned, they were telling me that my ambition and drive were vanity. I guess in the end though, maybe they *were* vanity?

It sure felt like it to me; I mean, 300 interviews of insanely awesome people, traveling all over the country, taking notes of timeless wisdom—all this work, and it felt like I'd accomplished nothing that really mattered.

Over the next few days, my thoughts turned back to the words of a man I'd interviewed a couple months prior: Mark Whitacre, the former executive of a multi-billion dollar company who had once served as an FBI whistleblower, and who was later found out in 1998 for his embezzlement of $9,000,000 and forced to spend eight years in federal prison. In fact, the story is so wild that there was a movie made about it called *The Informant*, starring actor Matt Damon.

Today, Mark is an active speaker and broadcaster of the message he learned through his entire wild experience, which is, as he told me, "If you're searching for money or power, it will never be enough—trust me, I've tried. A life of significance, which is about others, is so much more rewarding than a life of success, which is just about you."

I hadn't bought Mark's words at first, and remember thinking in annoyance, "*There it is again. Some wise guru saying the pursuit of wealth and power is futile…*" But now, as I recalled his words and mulled them over, I realized the truth of why Joe White and John Maxwell pushed themselves beyond what made sense for their own gain and comfort.

It's from people like Joe and John that I've come to learn life is meant to be an adventure through and through, not simply efficient in the beginning and boring in the end. Most people look for satisfaction and fulfillment in their long sought-after destination, in *success*. But what I've come to learn is that a truly worthwhile life isn't found in success—it's found in something bigger than that.

Yes, both Joe White and John Maxwell certainly could be retired, but life is about more than that for them. They aren't tearing it up at age seventy in order to continue getting stuff; no, they learned long ago that that pursuit only leaves you starved. But they also aren't settling for "enough," as so many others seem to do.

Tell me, at what point have you made enough of an impact on the world? At what point have you made enough of a difference? At what point have you had enough of Christ? I know of no limit.

What I've since come to learn is that ambition, drive, and resolve are not vanity. Rather, using them for no greater purpose than your own gain is vanity. It's like owning a $50,000 camera and only using it to take selfies.

I challenge you, call upon every last ounce of ambition, drive, resolve, passion, and power surging through your body. Utterly kill it in life and hold nothing back. Dare to fight and live for so much more than just yourself, because you cannot fill yourself with enough stuff to make yourself come alive and make life worthwhile. To fully come alive, you have to live because you love the journey, not just because you want what's at the end.

I remember talking with my grandfather on my dad's side of the family once in the lodge at our family's ranch. I asked him to share one of the biggest things he'd learned in life, that he wanted to impart to me and our family's future generations. He thought for a moment and then said, "Holden, enjoy life as you go along, or you'll get to the end of it with white hair and be too late."

When I'm my grandfather's age and my hair is as silvery white as his, I want to be able to tell my grandchildren the same thing. I want to inspire them by the way I've lived my life and by the way I've taken risks to use all I've been given to love others, and to love my Creator. I want to be living proof that life isn't about holding onto everything you have—it's about holding nothing back.

In the end, it's your choice: Do you want to be left hungry after consuming all you can for yourself, or do you want to stay hungry to give life everything you've got for others?

Chapter 7

BE BRAVE

"Chase the lion—if you run away, you'll be running the rest of your life."

—Mark Batterson,
pastor and author, interview #470

I'm probably like most people in the sense that I can't remember a whole lot of specific events and details about my early childhood. There is one event that occurred when I was seven, however, that I couldn't possibly forget.

My family and I were on vacation at the beach, and all of us were outside enjoying the day. I was walking along the shoreline and came upon an ancient lava flow with lava rocks and sand pits competing for space. The rocks jutted into the water and formed a reef both above and below its surface.

I was mesmerized by the raging waves as they rolled in, crashed, and splintered against the edge of the reef, engulfing everything in a brilliant spray of saltwater. The feeling of the mist exploding against me was amazing, and as I basked in the smell of the ocean and the feel of the sand under my feet, I found myself in awe of the vast expanse of water reaching out to the horizon. I loved everything about it and wanted to be closer to it.

My mom had been walking with me up until a few minutes ago, but now trailed behind, watching me collect seashells and poke sea urchins with them. Everything looked wonderful: the rolling gentle sea, her son enjoying God's world—even the jagged lava rock that I played on held an element of dangerous beauty.

But then, her bliss was replaced with a sudden, unmistakable urgency that swept through her body: *"Holden needs to move."*

"Holden, come here!" my mom yelled, calling me to come back toward her. But I didn't listen. I was too immersed in poking sea urchins.

My mom watched me expectantly for a moment, waiting for me to come. She saw nothing out of the ordinary, but her dread wasn't based on what she saw. And when I refused to listen, the urgent voice returned at ten times the intensity and roared inside my mom's mind, *"Tell Holden to move, NOW!"*

Just after finding myself another seashell, I suddenly heard my mom desperately scream my name to run away from the reef. Finally catching the life-and-death in her voice, I turned away from the ocean and took two steps up the shore—just in time by milliseconds.

At that moment an abnormally large wave, much bigger than any from earlier that day, rolled in that had so far been hidden among the other countless swells. Rather than just crashing against the rocks and breaking apart, this monster crashed over the top of the rocks and flooded over the lava flow—and me—with several feet of water.

I was instantly knocked off my feet and plunged into the swirling tide like laundry in a washing machine. I knew how to swim, but trying to do so felt impossible as I floundered around, eyes clenched tight and holding my breath. And just as I thought I'd be able to escape the turbulent water, the wave started pulling back out—me with it.

Thanks to the two steps I'd taken up shore, I had a few seconds to go before the wave finished sucking me off the top of the reef and down onto the jagged igneous rock below. Still submerged under water, I frantically began clawing beneath me for something to grab, but only wet, silky sand slipped through my fingers.

Then I felt my legs, then my stomach, and then my entire chest scrape against a bed of sharp lava rock, and I knew I only had one chance. Thrusting my hands toward the jagged surface, I grabbed hold, my mind racing too fast to notice any pain. As the receding wave washed over me, I held fast to the rocky ledge above the lower reef and stumbled back to my feet. Sputtering seawater and scraped from head to foot, I ran back up the shore to my mother's arms just as the next wave crashed—the one that would have blasted me to pieces.

As a boy, I grew up hardly scared of anything, and that day on the lava flow only strengthened my resolve. I don't know how to explain it, but even at seven years old I was aware of bigger powers at work than those which I could see. I knew it wasn't just my mother's voice that saved me, nor the lava rock I "happened" to find, nor the grip of my own two hands. Without a doubt, I knew God saved me that day, and I knew that if God could save me from the sea, he could save me from anything.

However, as I grew older and I began to develop a thirst for popularity, that all changed. I'd been raised with a spirit of confidence and adventure for God's glory, but as a teenager, I began to see those gifts as an opportunity for my glory. And so the game began: impress people daily, make myself look wild and fearless, make people want to be me, and build the perfect image for myself so people think I'm amazing.

On one hand, it worked. Labels like "fearless," "bold," and "risk taker" eventually became my identity, and on the outside I looked the part. But my persona failed where it counted because on the inside, I didn't even know who I was. I pushed myself to the ends of the earth to appear scared of nothing, but really, the reason I pushed myself so far to appear audacious was that deep down, I was scared to death of people rejecting me.

One thing I've learned about fearlessness is that sometimes, even the bravest-looking people in the world are complete cowards. It just so happens that with certain people, the way in which they run from their fear can sometimes look daring to the rest of us.

Lion Chaser

It was 3 a.m. one morning in February of 2016, and I was sitting in the window seat of a plane currently in takeoff for Washington, DC, with Dad seated on my left. I was going to DC because of a number of interviews I had lined up, and Dad was going in order to help his best friend from college, whom I call Uncle Rick, run our company's booth at a convention.

My eyes had felt groggy only seconds ago, but now, as the plane fired its engines, flashed its exterior lights, and exploded down the runway, I was wide awake. Adrenaline and excitement coursed through my veins. As a child, I always relished the feeling of a plane taking flight, and I guess it's one giddy pleasure I may never grow out of.

Staring out the plane window, eyes wide open and a grin splitting my face, I was pulled into deep thought as the runway lights flashed across the view of my window. Crazy, wasn't it? That right now, I was on a flight bound for Washington, DC for my interview journey.

And it was crazy that I was fewer than forty interviews away from finishing the 500. Crazy that among the other high-caliber leaders I was meeting with in Washington, I also had thirty minutes scheduled with pastor and *New York Times* bestselling author Mark Batterson. Crazy, wasn't it, that everything I was doing now was once started by some scared, insecure, people-pleasing teenager from Edmond, Oklahoma?

Yes, it was crazy. What was even crazier was the realization that a year and a half ago, sitting on this flight bound for DC in order to speak with and learn from national leaders like Mark Batterson would have terrified me. But now, there was hardly an ounce of fear in me. At least, it was all crazy to me.

In what felt like no time at all, we touched down in DC and took a cab to meet up with Uncle Rick outside our hotel. Since I didn't have any interviews until the next day, I decided to help Dad and Uncle Rick network the convention. So after a few hours of sightseeing, we lugged all our stuff over to the venue and set up our booth—no chairs, though. As Uncle Rick told me, "Chairs would just get in the way. We go to conventions to engage with people, not watch them walk by."

When we left the convention at the end of the day, our feet were killing us. Given the fact we were somewhere as amazing as Washington, DC, and also to reward ourselves for a solid first day at the convention, we opted to find somewhere cool to eat dinner. Before long, I found myself squeezed in at a table in an Irish pub, cracking jokes with Dad and Uncle Rick, who held authentic frothing beer mugs. Considering the half-empty Root Beer bottle I held in my hand, I felt like a wiener in a steakhouse.

After our food came out and we prayed, Uncle Rick took a look at the two men who had just recently been seated behind me—a bald man and an older man with a long twisted mustache. After a moment of looking at them, Uncle Rick looked at me and said, "Holden, ask the bald man behind you if he's the guy on Fox News."

Confused, I gave Uncle Rick a puzzled look. He leaned in and elaborated, "I swear I've seen him on Megyn Kelly's show before. I don't remember his name, but I think he's one of the commentators. Just ask him." I shrugged and turned around.

"Hey, gentlemen!" I addressed them both. Then I said to the younger, bald man, "Sir, we were just wondering if you're the guy from Fox News?"

The man smiled broadly and exclaimed, "I sure am!" I brought my arm around and stuck my hand out, matching his excited smile. "I'm Holden! I'm sorry, but we couldn't recall your name," I said expectantly, nodding my head back toward Dad and Uncle Rick. He took my hand and said to all of us, "I'm Arthur. Arthur Aidala. Nice to meet you all!"

The morning after meeting Arthur, I donned a pair of blue jeans, black alligator cowboy boots, one of my usual black "interview" shirts, and a gray sports jacket. I didn't normally dress up to the extent of wearing a jacket, but hey, today was the day I was meeting Mark Batterson.

Mark had requested for us to meet him at his office, located directly above his church's famous coffee shop Ebenezer's, so that's what we did. Arriving a few minutes early, we hung out in Ebenezer's for a little bit before being shown upstairs to the lobby outside Mark's office.

When Mark finally came out of his office, having just finished a meeting with two other gentlemen, I greeted him with the broad, excited grin that by now had become a kind of trademark of mine, and I shook his hand. Somehow, in an instant he made me feel like we'd been good friends for forever.

After my allotted thirty minutes of gutting Mr. Batterson for wisdom, I asked him the one question I almost always asked as my closer: "If, when I walk out of here, I only learned one thing from you to share in the book I write at the end of my project, what one thing would you want that to be?"

A smile crossed my face. I knew how big a question this was, and I always found it fascinating to watch a person search for their answer to it. Mr. Batterson thought about it, and then matched my smile as he replied, "Chase the lion—if you run away, you'll be running the rest of your life."

I froze as his words reverberated in my mind, and then attacked my journal with my pen to jot down the quote and his explanation. But for me, the quote needed no explanation. I knew exactly what he meant.

Own The Moment

As stunningly beautiful as I think lions are, I'm rather glad I've never stumbled upon one in the wild—I like my arms and legs the way they are. But Mr. Batterson hadn't necessarily been talking about the large African cat. A lion, as far as Mr. Batterson had meant it, was anything that scared you.

It's the skateboard trick you're scared to try, because what if you get hurt?

It's the friendship you're scared to initiate, because what if they don't like you?

It's the dream, whatever that dream is, that you're afraid to pursue, because what if you fail?

Or, in my case, it's the person I feel called to be but am afraid to become, because what if people reject me and I become an outcast?

I've spent my whole life waging a civil war in my mind between fear and God-given desire. *"Will I run and hide, or will I face what I'm afraid of and brave the tide? Will I challenge the seas and dare to set sail, or will I stay in the harbor and rust for fear I might fail? Will I buckle under pressure and retreat to what's safe, or will I flex my back and stand in faith?"*

In the end, I've come to find that the longer you run and hide from something, the more afraid of it you will become. The more you try to fit in, the more afraid of standing out you will become. The more you try to avoid failure, the more scared of failing you will become. The more you let safety and security determine your trajectory in life, the more afraid of stepping out in faith you will become. You cannot outrun the lions that fear manifests itself as.

To break fear, you have to face what scares you. One man who talked to me about this was Scott Hamilton, the US and World Champion figure skater who won the gold medal in the 1984 Olympics. Mr. Hamilton told me, "When you fail, you learn what it feels like to lose. By experiencing that disappointment, you not only learn that you don't want to do that again, but you also aren't afraid of it anymore. You're free to work harder for the next time because you already know failure hurts, but it's not fatal."

In many ways, bravery is like diving off a waterside cliff. The ground you stand on is safe, and the fall to the water beneath is daunting. But the more often you force yourself to jump, the less afraid you become. There's no way to outrun fear or go around it—the only way is through it, and once you take the first step and let your feet leave the ground, all the fear washes away.

I'm nothing special when it comes to cliff jumping, but through my amateur experience, I've learned how to break fear's grip: *seize the moment, and just jump.* Don't think about hitting the water, just simply focus on making your feet leave the ground.

You should always be guided by wisdom, but never allow yourself to be broken by fear. For when fear breaks you once, it will be easier for it to break you next time. The more often you let yourself get away with being afraid, the tighter it will grip you. Alternatively, the more you push yourself to break fear, the weaker its hold on you will be.

I once had the chance to meet and talk with Max McClean, a theatrical producer and actor from New York City, after he had just staged a version of C.S. Lewis' *Screwtape Letters.* I'd asked him how he finds courage in the face of so many people watching him on stage, and Mr. McClean had responded, "Backstage I'm filled with anxiety, but when I force myself to step out on stage, all the fear vanishes."

Don't overthink it or try to figure it all out, *just jump.* Own the moment and force yourself to breach the point of no return.

Chase what scares you—chase the dreams that scare you, chase the challenges that scare you. If you let yourself run away, you'll be running the rest of your life. You get to decide the man or woman you become, and whether you become a warrior or a coward. And you determine that by each decision you make.

The jump you face right now is about something much bigger than a cheap thrill or a cool Instagram picture—it's about the man or woman you are choosing to become.

As you grow up, you get to decide: Do I want to grow brave, or grow tired? And one thing I know for sure is that you'll never grow brave by running away.

Be You

When I was talking with Christine Caine—the international speaker, author, and activist—one thing I asked her was, "What is it that holds people back from going all in for life? From jumping into the adventure of life and giving it everything they've got? What causes them to just drift through life rather than kill it?"

Her answer came almost before I was done with my question. She looked me in the eyes, her own eyes glinting, and said in her Australian accent, "It's fear! It's focusing on 'what if this or that happens?' And here's what you need to remember: to overcome fear, you have to make what you do know about God bigger than what you don't know about the future."

I let a grin cross my face as she continued. I loved it when a person was passionate about their answer, not merely educated in it.

"And the second thing," she added, "is human nature. If you do not aggressively disrupt your human nature with risk and action, you will default back to comfort and complacency. The degree to which you will allow yourself to be interrupted or inconvenienced is the degree to which God will do something powerful through your life."

As soon as she finished talking, I jumped to my follow-up question. "If it's fear that holds so many people back, then what's it take to live fearless?"

And that's when she told me something I'll never forget. She answered, "It's not as romantic as it seems. Living fearless and living reckless are two very different things. Fearless living is 'I'm going to go counter-culture, regardless of the consequences.' Reckless living is often 'I'm just going to do this because it's cool.' In fact, it can be quite the contrary of fearless living, because you can be more accepted by being cool, being a rebel, and being on the edge that way." Then she added with a wink, "It takes more than skinny jeans and tattoos to change the world."

I laughed, and she did, too, as she exclaimed, "You can quote me on that!"

There's a difference between fearlessness and recklessness, and a difference between confidence and arrogance. I know, because I've been all of them. Fearlessness and confidence are the results of knowing who you are, while recklessness and arrogance are the results of not knowing who you are.

I used to rely on other people to tell me who I was: that I was adventurous, that I was confident, that I was a risk taker. But deep down, though I knew I wanted to be those things, I knew I was a fake. Not because my actions didn't look brave, and not because my stride didn't look confident. Yeah, I sure tried to look like I had it all together—I acted like it, and I told myself that I did. But fearlessness and confidence aren't about what it looks like on the outside. I was a fake not because my appearance didn't match my persona, but because my heart didn't.

I acted fearless to run from my fear, and I acted confident to hide my insecurity. And that meant that I was willing to morph my character into whatever it needed to be for me to keep up my false identity. Fake. Disgustingly fake.

It was as fake a substitute for identity as lust is a fake substitute for love. The difference? It's not the actions and image. Lust and love may look the same on the outside in many ways, just as recklessness and fearlessness may often look similar. The difference is in the heart.

Maybe you've searched for identity differently than I have. Maybe your search for identity hasn't led you to daredevil stunts. Maybe instead, you've turned to gossip to elevate yourself, or maybe you've traded your body in exchange for cheap attention. Maybe you've applied your mind or athletic ability just to gain the infatuation of others. I guess we can all find a plastic identity in a perversion of the gifts God has given us. I don't know how you're inclined to alter yourself for a sense of identity, but I do know one thing: you'll never break fear by acting like someone else.

To be fearless, you have to be you.

No matter what the immediate result of your decision might be, even if it's something really small like introducing yourself to someone or sending a text, never let yourself become a coward. Every moment of every day, you are choosing who you become, because becoming brave is just as much about the small decisions as it is the big decisions. As I've heard my pastor, Craig Groeschel, say, "The decisions we make today determine the story we tell tomorrow."

What story do you want to tell? What legacy do you want to leave? As you grow older, do you want to grow strong, or do you want to grow tired?

You can't chase both certainty and adventure. You cannot step out in faith with absolute certainty in where you're stepping. If you were absolutely certain about where you were going, it wouldn't be a step of faith, would it?

You get to decide: Does the enticement of security draw you more, or does the wild call of your heart draw you more? Does comfort draw you more, or does purpose draw you more? Do you prefer the comfort of safety, or the adventure of faith?

Just remember: brave isn't a feeling you get—it's the person you choose to be *right now*.

Chapter 8

WARRIOR

"Every time I go on stage and every time I'm afraid, I pray this prayer: 'Breathe through me, God.'"

—Sadie Robertson,
actress, motivational speaker, interview #486

"Hey what's up, everyone!" I exclaimed as I jogged toward the array of ENO-brand hammocks hanging from trees in our local city park. It was summer of 2016. I had just come from the lake and was barefoot in a pair of boardshorts and a HE>i tank top.

"Hey, Holden!" came the voice of my new friend Mikaela, an absolutely phenomenal singer, as she peeked over the top of her hammock. The other three high schoolers there gave me a smile and said "hey" back as I approached.

These were student leaders from several different high schools in Edmond, Oklahoma, that Mikaela had rallied together to help in the process of putting on the Edmond High School Worship Night, which hundreds of high school students from Edmond and beyond attended every year. But at the time, I had never attended one of these Worship Nights before and had no idea how big and impactful it was.

Over the past few months, I had released a few YouTube vlogs of me sharing thoughts I had, stories I'd lived out, and lessons I'd learned. They weren't very good in my opinion, but if being an inspiring and compelling communicator was something I wanted to become, I knew starting poorly and with YouTube was my first step: start where you are with what you have.

However, for some reason, my vlogs had really started catching fire and circulating around my friend groups and beyond. Before long, Mikaela had gotten wind of them. After watching one of my videos, she apparently had been impressed by what I had to share, and, in anticipation of the worship event she was planning at the beginning of the school year, had decided to reach out to me about speaking at it.

That's what this "hammock meeting" at Hafer Park was about—the upcoming high school worship night. When Mikaela had first reached out to me about being the speaker of the night, I hadn't thought much about it. She hadn't really shared any details with me, just that she wanted me to speak at a worship event she was part of putting on.

However, after our hammock meeting was over and now that I had a better understanding of the details and magnitude of what Worship Night entailed, I was left reeling. In years past, there had consistently been several hundred teens attending Worship Night from all across Oklahoma—and this time they were expecting the group to be even bigger. Mikaela was the lead singer, and I was supposed to be the keynote speaker.

At first, I felt honored to be asked and was staggeringly excited about it. I'd given speeches before—either at family-and-friends events or alongside my dad—so even though I'd never spoken at an official event by myself, I was confident I had what it took. The theme for the night and the topic I was supposed to speak on was "All In," which I knew I could talk about in my sleep. I spent some time working on my speech one of the first days that week, and had it pretty nailed down in an hour.

But somehow, fear still managed to penetrate my mind, taunting me with whispers of doubt. *"How are you going to measure up to all the other speakers Mikaela could have asked? How are you going to measure up to the speakers you've interviewed? How are you going to measure up to Lecrae, Craig Groeschel, Dave Ramsey, or heck, even someone like Sadie Robertson, who is close to your own age?"*

With some work, I managed to cast my doubt aside as I had learned to do so many times before. The doubt I felt wasn't real; it was just fear talking.

However, after a couple months of feeling like a high-roller, doubt swept over me again, and this time it was actually well-founded: the leadership committee of Worship Night had decided to change the theme of the night and, therefore, the topic I was speaking on. Now, instead of the theme being "All In," it was "Even When."

If that makes sense to you right off the bat, congratulations, but I swear I didn't have the slightest clue as to what it meant. I spent the next month and a half grueling over the theme with prayer and thought as I tried to figure out what it meant to me, but I came up blank. I mean, I could give a plastic response on what I guessed it could mean to other people, but no matter how hard I tried or how deep I thought, I couldn't understand what significance the words "even when" held for *me*. I might as well have been asked to speak on a theme of "Orange T-Shirts" or "Dishwashers."

Eventually, I got to a point one evening when I realized I was going to have to abandon Worship Night. How was I supposed to speak on a topic that I didn't even know if I believed in? Well, I couldn't, and that was that. Admitting defeat, I pulled my phone out of my pocket and went to Mikaela's contact, but just before I called her, a thought shot into my mind: *"Holden, do you really think God gave this opportunity to you for the heck of it? So you could just throw it aside?"*

My thumb was left hovering over the call button as I considered the thought. *"Oh I get it, you speak in third person sometimes, too."* I shot the thought at God with a tinge of bitter sarcasm, spiteful that he had the audacity to question my resolve but wouldn't even give me the wisdom to understand what "Even When" meant.

Then suddenly, more thoughts started to stream into my mind: I sure liked shooting my mouth off about trusting God and stepping out in faith. Did I actually have the strength to do it? Was I an authentic horseman, or was I "all hat and no cattle?"

I prayed every single day that God would give me the spirit and courageous heart of a warrior. Did I actually mean what I prayed, or did I just like listening to myself talk? After a moment, I made up my mind, and I prayed, *"God, even when I don't know what to say, even when I don't know how I'm going to do it, and even when I'm scared, I'll go where you call me."*

After that, I laughed. I could hardly believe what I'd just prayed: "God, *even when…*" I took a deep breath and grabbed my laptop to begin a new speech preparation document. *"So that's what 'even when' means,"* I thought with a smile, and then reminded myself, *"I can do all things through Christ who strengthens me."*

Little did I know, this particular battle with fear had merely reached halftime.

The Source

It was two hours before Worship Night, and I had just exited off the turnpike and was making my way toward the church where we were holding the event. Six weeks earlier, when I had finally had my breakthrough as to what "Even When" meant, I'd thought I'd finally gotten it all figured out.

After that, it hadn't taken me long to forge a message, think of several stories, and develop some good points to structure my speech around. Honestly, from any other person's perspective, I would have appeared set. But I didn't feel like it. For some reason, something had felt off—like a very core element of my message was fake or wrong.

A month ago we had a rehearsal for Worship Night where I had delivered my speech, and afterward I'd been lavished with encouragement for how good it was. But the feeling of something being critically wrong had only intensified. The same had gone for my second rehearsal of it. And before I knew it, it was now two hours before open doors for Worship Night, and despite all the work I'd put into my speech over the past few weeks, it felt more fake and wrong now than ever before.

Before pulling into the Worship Night venue parking lot, I stopped at a gas station and grabbed a Red Bull; I was dead tired and would need the energy spike. I was supposed to have arrived at Worship Night at 4 p.m.—two hours earlier—but had been meeting with our family friend Corey Harouff, the YoungLife director of South Dakota, for the past few hours in order to help clear my mind.

Talking with Corey had helped me some regarding the tactical delivery of my speech, but the problem I felt at the core of my message hadn't budged an inch. Just to make matters worse, I now had a throbbing headache, tired eyelids, and a sick stomach. They were all most likely due to the minor anxiety attacks I was fighting off.

As much as I wanted to drink the Red Bull right then, I knew that the sugar rush would only last for a little bit, and that after it passed, I would have an energy plummet. I was going to have to time this carefully and drink the can right before I went on stage, or I would end up worse off than I was now.

When I finally dragged myself into the church where everyone was setting up, I stumbled over to my friend Kate, who was on the leadership board, and informed her I wasn't feeling well.

She gave me one look and said, "Yeah, I can tell." Then, after thinking for a second, she continued, "There's a couch upstairs. If you want, you can crash there for a little bit, but don't take too long. We need you down here."

I nodded and then crawled up the staircase, shuffled into the room Kate had been talking about, and collapsed onto the padded bench she had referred to as a "couch." Before shutting my eyes, I retrieved my phone to check the progress on my last-ditch effort—well, other than Red Bull.

I was waiting to hear back from a friend and mentor of mine— Ray Sanders—on whether he would be able to come meet me at the church and help me figure out my problem. Sure enough, the text I'd just received from him said he would be on his way soon.

Thirty minutes later, I rolled my eyes open to the sound of my phone ringing—Mr. Sanders was calling to tell me he had arrived. I groaned and forced myself to my feet. Not that Mr. Sanders had woken me up or anything, because in those thirty minutes, I'd barely even been able to calm my frantic thinking, let alone sleep.

When I got downstairs, I greeted Mr. Sanders with a forced smile and directed him to a secluded area in the lobby. I kept calm, but didn't bother trying to hide the fact that I was in a real predicament. After telling him I felt like there was something critically wrong with the speech I was about to deliver and asking for his advice, I briefed him on the content of my speech and what I wanted to accomplish through it.

Even as the words came out of my mouth, I recognized how fake they sounded, but I couldn't determine why. We talked for a minute. Then, after thinking about it, Mr. Sanders replied, "Holden, this is amazing stuff, and it's true. But it doesn't sound like you."

I rolled my eyes with sarcasm as I thought, *"Well, no way."* Mr. Sanders didn't notice and continued talking.

"It has God in it, but not tied directly in. It sounds like something I'd hear from a secular motivational speaker, which is great, but it doesn't sound like *you*. I think that's your problem."

I froze—my sarcastic attitude replaced with a sense of sudden understanding. A million calculations ran through my mind all at once, and in an instant, I knew what Ray had just told me was exactly true. My entire speech was built on worldly ways I knew of to build the strength and courage needed to fight through struggles or challenges, "even when" you're tired and ready to give up.

I started thinking, *"Yes, I find strength by focusing more on the end goal than on the present struggle ... and yes, I find courage by facing what scares me rather than running from it ... and yes, I should talk about those two things like I was planning to. But were those two lessons, and many others I'd learned like them, really the essence of my strength and courage?"*

I knew the answer to that in a heartbeat.

No, they weren't the ultimate source, and neither was any other method I'd learned about building strength and courage. For me, the ultimate source was God.

I looked at Mr. Sanders, a spark in my eye, and said, "You're right." After a quick moment of thinking, I reached down to my backpack and retrieved my Red Bull, unopened and still cold. "And I think I know what to do about that."

Ten minutes later I was greeting people as they entered the doors of Worship Night. Thirty minutes later, Mikaela let loose the first words of *Even When it Hurts* by Hillsong, and an hour later I strode onto stage, my GoPro in my left hand and the still unopened Red Bull in my right, which I placed on the stool that had been set up for me as a podium of sorts. So much for drinking it prior to stage time.

The band played softly behind me, a sea of people looked up at me, and there I stood on the front of the stage where I was expected to say something meaningful. I held my tongue for a moment, feeling almost as if I were looking at myself from out in the crowd, and then silently recited a brief prayer I'd grown accustomed to over the past few months: *"Father, breathe through me."* Then I began.

My words were slow and reserved at first as I rationed my remaining energy into each sentence, but soon an energy reserve I hadn't been able to tap into earlier started feeding into my body. My mind electrified, my vision became vivid, my thoughts sharpened, and my muscles woke up—all effects of Red Bull, yes, but the 355 mL can remained unopened.

By the final quarter of my twenty-minute speech, I was pacing the length of the stage, mic held tight in my grip as I spit passion into it and let it boom out of the speakers all around me. I felt as fully alive as I could ever remember feeling. As I started to wrap up my talk, I turned to the Red Bull can still on the stool and grabbed it. After using it as a prop in a story I was telling, I took a sip of it and kept it in my hand. I had a point to make.

"And even when I have no idea how I'm going to make it," I began speaking, "how I'm going to overcome, how I could conquer my fear, or even when I have no idea what I'm going to talk about tonight or how I'm going to impact anybody—even when, fill in the blank—I'm going to grit my teeth and I'm going to *go* and seize the opportunity. You better believe nothing's going to hold me back, because…" I paused, and let a smirk cross my face as I rotated the Red Bull in my hand so the audience could see it clearly.

"The strength of Red Bull wears off, and so does every other source except one, and that is: you can do all things, not through Red Bull, *but through Christ who strengthens you.*"

That was it. The audience erupted in cheer, and I knew my message had hit home. But what was funny was that while I stood on that stage having just shared a message on finding strength in God, really, it was something I myself was just beginning to learn.

Remember Who's with You

"I can do all things through Christ who strengthens me." I remind myself of that truth daily, but it's not something I've always understood. As a daredevil teenager, I've tried just about every way I can think of to beat fear. I've numbed fear, I've suppressed fear, I've hidden from fear, I've managed to look fearless, and with God alongside me, I've even broken fears that I never could have imagined breaking. However, I've never found a way to permanently vanquish fear.

Sometimes God does instill us with supernatural bravery, with complete and utter fearlessness, and I know from personal experience that it's intoxicating when he does. However, often it's not so dramatic. What I've come to find is that bravery is rarely a feeling we get. Most of the time, it's a decision we make every day by one simple choice: Will I trust God?

Trusting God 100% isn't something I usually "feel" like doing. When I'm scared, I usually feel like hiding, running, or clinging to the illusion of security. However, being brave isn't about how you feel, it's about what you decide.

Amy Groeschel, wife of Pastor Craig Groeschel and someone who is like another mother to me, once told me, "It's frightening to take risks. You feel like a child. I want to stay like a child. To seek, delight in, and cling to my Father." Fearlessness is a choice you make when you decide either to cling to your facades of security or to cling to God.

When I was talking with David Platt, an international pastor and evangelist, he told me, "We don't always know where we're going, but we always know who we're with." Fearlessness is a choice we make when we either stay where we feel safe, or go where we know God will be with us. You've got to make a choice to believe in God and believe that he's going to protect you, carry you through, and do things you could never do on your own.

As Rex Crain, my motivational speaker friend from California I've mentioned before, told me, "Miracles are the way God thinks. It's what he does. Walk with a miracle mentality." Live fearlessly, not because things aren't scary, but because you know who's with you.

Mark Batterson also drove this home to me during our interview when we discussed his book *Chase the Lion.* "If your dream doesn't scare you, it's too small," he said. I didn't fully understand what he meant at first, but over time and through one experience after another, I've come to see the truth. If your dream feels safe, it's too small. If your dream can be accomplished by just you, it's too small. If your dream doesn't scare you, you need a bigger dream because, in the end, bravery isn't gained by staying where it's safe, but by going where you're scared.

Eventually, you have to choose between the comfort of safety or the adventure of faith. You have to choose whether you'd rather live following the paths made by everyone else and walking in the center of the crowd—held captive to avoid danger and live dictated by fear—or live following the call of your heart, being different and moving against the crowd, living free to go where God leads you.

Like Wes Lane, a former District Attorney for the State of Oklahoma and the founder of Salt and Light Leadership Training (SALLT), would tell me, "My dad is the biggest, baddest bear in the woods, I'm his boy, and he has a mission for me." As it is, Wes was talking about his spiritual daddy. To be truly fearless, that's the mentality you have to get inside your head.

You have to reach the point where the thought of abandoning your calling, passions, and dreams in order to follow safety doesn't even appeal to you, because you know the biggest, baddest bear in the woods lives inside you and all around you, and he's protecting you.

Breathe Through Me

Several months prior to Worship Night, I was sitting in my bedroom on a wooden stump that I use for a chair, my phone in hand as I waited for a call, and my leather-bound journal on my bed open to a new page headlined "Sadie Robertson."

After my failed attempts at interviewing Willie Robertson of *Duck Dynasty*, I was about to talk to his daughter Sadie. A young adult like me, Sadie is the founder of her brand Live Original, a passionate nationwide speaker, an author, and ultimately, an inspiration and encouragement to the next generation—including myself.

Sadie was scheduled to call me at any minute. Fear's thoughts swirled on the fringes of my mind, subtly taunting me with memories of how I had botched things up when trying to reach out to Sadie's dad over a half-year earlier. *"Who are you to talk with Sadie? You don't have what it takes. Dude, don't you remember what happened last time you tried to talk with a Robertson?"*

But that's all fear could do: taunt me. It couldn't stop me this time. With a clenched jaw, I rejected the fear. Things were going to be different this time. This time, my mission wasn't to get a big, important, well-known name included in my book to make myself look more impressive. Not this time.

This time, it wasn't just about me. I was calling Sadie because I cared about *her,* because I believed in her, and because I believed that if I could challenge and push her in an interview, we would both leave our conversation more equipped to make a difference in the world. I solidified the thought in my mind and prayed to God saying, *"This is for you."*

At that moment, somehow, the commitment moved twelve inches down from my head and took root in my heart. It wasn't just something I thought in my mind anymore. It was something I truly believed to my core: this really was about something bigger than me. Funny, I'd made that commitment and change of heart before. The darn decision wouldn't stick. I guess sometimes, change is a process.

Finally, my phone started to ring with a call coming in from Monroe, Louisiana.

"This is Holden!" I said, answering the phone.

"Hey, this is Sadie!" came a familiar voice with a strong Louisiana accent. Odd that it was familiar, as I'd never met Sadie before. My family and I had probably watched a few too many *Duck Dynasty* episodes.

Sadie and I hit it off like old friends. She wanted to know all about me and my interview project, and I wanted to know all about her and her Live Original brand. Eventually, we got on the topic of fear and courage, and one of the things I asked her was how she fights fear. I'll never forget her answer. She said, "I pray this over and over all the time: *'Breathe through me, God.'"*

I knew in an instant what she meant. It was the same thing I had prayed before picking up the phone to talk with her, just in different words. Thirty minutes elapsed before we had to end the phone call, and when I put my phone down, the one thing still burning on the forefront of my mind was that statement Sadie had made: "Breathe through me, God."

I spoke with Sadie on April 26, 2016, and before then, whenever

I'd felt scared, weak, or empty, my prayer had always been, *"Father, give me strength and courage."* My prayer had been that, in the same way God had once breathed life into Adam, he breathed power and life into me.

However, after talking with Sadie that day, my prayer upgraded. Now, my prayer wasn't simply that God breathed life into me, but that he breathed *through* me.

At first, I didn't recognize the incredible power of that simple shift of focus. But as time passed, the change inside me made it impossible for me not to recognize it.

In the past, I had only relied on God whenever I had found myself short of breath: scared, weak, or empty. But now, my prayer was not only that God fill me when I couldn't handle things on my own, but that he would actually use and breathe through me to such an extent that there was *no way* I could handle things on my own. And as a result, I found myself leaning into him for strength and courage more than I'd ever dared to do before. Because what if when I allowed myself to fully lean into him, he was no longer there?

But as I discovered, he was there. And as I started truly relying on him, I started living from a source of more strength, courage, and life than I could have ever held in my own two lungs.

Love of a Warrior

There's a saying that goes, "I'm a lover, not a fighter." Maybe you've heard it. I don't know who came up with it, but it sure sounds good, doesn't it? I mean, it even rhymes. How cute. But here's what I want to know: if you aren't willing to fight, then how can you truly love?

There's another saying I know of that goes, "For God so loved the world, that He gave his only son, so that whoever believes in Him shall not perish but have eternal life" (John 3:16). I actually do know who came up with that saying, and I also know something about him:

he went to war against hell, fought evil itself, and conquered death because of how much he loves us.

True love, as far as I know it, isn't the greasy romance depicted by Hollywood or the watered-down quality of being "nice" we're taught by society. Let me ask you: Would you ever die for yourself? I mean, would you die to get something you've always wanted? I mean, would you die for a billion dollars? Would you die to gain the whole world?

No, you wouldn't, unless you're very confused about what the word 'dead' means. Now, let me ask you another question: Would you die for someone you dearly love? If you love them enough, then yes, you would. That kind of love—I mean true, raw, living love that you would die fighting for if necessary—is the essence of bravery.

Another member of the *Duck Dynasty* gang I had the chance to talk with in my journey of interviews was Korie Robertson, and I remember asking her one of the same questions I'd asked her daughter Sadie: "How do you break fear?" Her answer had been about as straightforward as they come. She'd said, "Realize it's not about you! Get the focus off yourself and onto others."

Bravery is as great as our love is strong, and that's why we're timid and weak when our love is constrained to ourselves. We would never die for our own skin, but we will fight to the death for those we dearly love, because as it's said in 1 John 4:18, "Perfect love casts out fear."

If you want to be fearless, fall in love.

Ultimately, love for the light doesn't come without a need to fight the darkness. Like a quote from C.S. Lewis that Max McClean, the theatrical producer from New York City, shared with me during our conversation says, "Courage is every virtue at its testing point."

Courage and fearlessness mean standing for what's right, fighting for what you love, and refusing to fall into the mold of safe living at the cost of compromising what you should stand and fight for. Fearlessness is about the willingness to stand against the culture and to split the current of people rushing past you—as tough and terrifying as it may be—because you refuse to trade your backbone of pride and heart of passion for a dull and meaningless life of safety and security. We love with valor and true grit, because as it's said in Romans 8:31, "If God is for us, who can be against us?"

We're born as children, and when we're born again in Christ, we're born as warriors—not because we're born to fight, but because we're born to love.

What are you brave for? Are you brave for an image? Are you brave for small ambitions? Or are you brave because you have the love of a warrior?

Chapter 9

WIDE AWAKE

"Don't treat now like it's nothing but a stepping stone to something better or something more. Seize the 'now' like it's the exact moment God made you for—because it very well may be."

—Bart Millard,
songwriter and lead singer of MercyMe, interview #498

"Over this past year, I actually had two friends of mine pass away. One died in a horrible four-wheeler accident, and the other took his own life..."

My friend Anna and I were on stage in front of a group of several hundred students. She was the one talking, her words measured and deliberate, and I stood quietly next to her, listening as she addressed the massive crowd.

We were campaigning for president and vice president of a youth leadership camp known as TeenPact, and were addressing the mock-political party we were running in. At the moment, we were sharing our hearts on the message we wanted to broadcast that week, a message printed boldly on the front of the t-shirts we were wearing: "Liv'n to Kill it." On the sleeve of each shirt, our names were also printed: "Holden Hill and Anna Groeschel for President/VP 2K16." The audience was flooded with our voting base wearing the same shirt.

Earlier that morning, Anna had come to me and said she had a particular story she felt called to share during the speech we were planning to give that afternoon. I'd asked her what it was she wanted to share, but she'd said she couldn't tell me because she wanted to save her composure for when she really needed it—and now I knew what she'd meant. I'd known of both the high school students Anna was talking about, but hadn't known them personally like she had. Though Anna is as tough as nails and you would never know it, the death of those friends had been extremely hard for her.

"So livin' to kill it, like we're talking about, reminds us that we each have one life in which we get to do everything according and unto Christ," Anna said as she continued to address the crowd of teens, "and one person who did that tremendously was my dear friend Colton who got in the horrible accident. What I've learned as a result of that is how important it is to seize the life we have and make the most of it."

When Anna had first started speaking, getting the words out had been kind of hard for her, but now they were full of passion and power as her presence owned the stage.

"If we don't step out and live to the full potential that Christ has given us, we're not killin' it, we're just living safely. And so I encourage you to live to your full potential, because I hope you remember, you only have one life to live."

With that, she let her arm fall to her side. She had just totally dominated everything I or anyone else on that stage had said prior to her. Having spoken just before her, I'd been the one to hand her the mic and had thought my speech had gone pretty well—that is, until Anna made it sound like a child's story book compared to the heartfelt epic she had just shared with our audience. The auditorium erupted with applause, but I barely heard it. I was too deep in thought about what Anna had said.

Later that day, all of the students from every political party at camp voted for their candidates. Despite our rigorous campaign, we ended up losing the primary election by a slim margin to two other friends of ours running against us. They would go on to campaign for office in the general election throughout the week, and Anna and I were now done.

As soon as the announcement was made, my confidence imploded. I truly believed God had been leading me and Anna to run this race, which is why I had asked her to run alongside me as Vice President. Now, it was all over before it had even really begun. But then, I had an idea: *"Boy, you forgot that the point of all this wasn't to get elected, it was to impact people. You may not be able to win presidency anymore, but you can still share the message. Maybe if you talk with Anna and get her on board..."*

The thought trailed off, and I winced as a tinge of fear shot through my body and started trash-talking my willpower. *"You didn't have what it takes to get elected, so what makes you think you have what it takes to share your dumb message now that you aren't even on stage anymore? Oh, that's right, everyone thinks it's a dumb message—if they'd liked it, they would have voted for it. Ha! And you know what, you're talking about 'killing it' and you couldn't even make it past the presidential primary election of a youth camp. Maybe Anna should have run alongside someone else... because you let her down."*

My willpower retreated at fear's mocking sneer, and I sunk deeper into my auditorium chair as the camp announcer continued to talk about something. I have no idea what—I wasn't paying attention. I went quiet for the remainder of the time we spent in that large auditorium listening to election results, speakers, and event updates for the evening.

Eventually, we were released to sports events and free time, and I spent the rest of the day taking down campaign posters and feeling beaten. However, by that evening I finally worked up the courage to mention my idea to Anna. Well, I say I worked up the courage—more like I worked up the "I don't give a rip if I fail so long as I get this off my mind."

It was an hour before bedtime curfew, and all the camp students were hanging around snack tables in a big open park. I started looking around for Anna's brown hair, and upon finally spotting her among the crowd, yelled her name.

"Hey, Anna!"

She turned as I fought my way through the crowd and ran up to her.

"What's up?" she asked.

I collected my thoughts real quick and then proceeded, too caught up in the moment to give a second thought to fear screaming "Loser!" at me through the back of my skull.

"Our message is livin' to kill it. You said in your speech that we have one life to live, and anything less than that is just living safely. Living safe isn't killing it, it's hiding."

She nodded as she gave her response. "Yeah. What about it?"

"Well, if we quit now, that's just playing it safe and taking it easy. Who says we can't still share our message and start a movement, regardless of the fact we didn't get elected? Who says we have to give up? I refuse to get beat. We came here to talk about killing it; let's actually do it. We've got a message to share."

Her eyes glinted. She paused a moment, and then nodded her head slowly and deliberately. "Let's do it! You're right: we didn't come here necessarily to get elected, we came here to make a difference. Let's get this message out there," she said with a grin and a knowing tone in her voice.

With Anna now on board with me, my entire attitude whirled 180 degrees. Fearlessness and confidence exploded through my body again, and I felt a sense of passion and purpose greater than I'd felt at any point during my ambitious campaign for presidency. Resolve steeled my backbone and lifted the corner of my mouth in a smirk.

From the outside in, our efforts may have looked limited since we didn't have the stage anymore, but Anna and I both knew the unspoken truth: God had led us here, and so long as we had him, we didn't need the stage.

Through every situation, opportunity, and interaction that week, we spread our vision like wildfire, instilling it further in the hearts of friends and everyone we met. We challenged them with our words and inspired them with our actions. By the end of that week, our message had come to reverberate across camp, and especially in me—a message that screamed "Live wide awake, because you don't get to live twice."

No Time For Caution

Be safe, or you might get scraped up.

Be careful, or you might mess up.

Don't get too attached to someone, or you might get hurt in the end.

Stay close to home, because traveling long distances isn't safe.

Don't try something before you know it works, or you'll get made fun of.

Don't stand up for people, and definitely not people who haven't already done something for you, or you'll risk becoming an outcast.

Don't speak your mind, because some people may disagree with you.

Don't attempt anything you haven't already done, because you might embarrass yourself.

Don't run for president of a youth camp, and once you lose, definitely don't get back up and keep fighting on, because you'll just fail even harder.

That's what we're told to do. What a miserable way to live and die.

In January of 2016 I was sitting in my dad's office, my phone pressed against my cheek as I talked with Michael Jr., the comedian and actor from California. Over the past few months, I'd become rather familiar with Michael, having attended a conference he'd performed at, watched his content on YouTube, and heard him speak at my church.

Then, just a few weeks earlier, I'd watched the movie *War Room*, which Michael stars in, and that did it for me—it was high time I reached out to him about an interview. I contacted his press team, and after a few weeks' worth of email conversation with them, here Michael and I were with fifteen minutes on the phone, having a blast and talking away.

One of the questions I asked Michael toward the end of our conversation was, "What's one of the most important lessons you've learned in life—something that would accelerate the growth and impact of young people like me if we learn it early on?"

It didn't take Michael long to decide on his answer. After a quick pause, he proceeded, "You know, everyone is asking what they can get out of life. When people walk into a store they're saying, 'What can I get?' When they enter a relationship, they're asking, 'What's in it for me?' When they go into church, they're asking, 'What will this do for me?'"

Now interested, I went to work taking notes on what he was saying. Michael continued.

"The biggest thing I've found that has been a breakthrough for my career is simply to make the shift and ask, 'What can I give?' One night at a club, instead of asking 'How can I get laughs from the audience?' I simply started asking myself 'How can I give them the opportunity to laugh?' And that shift right there changed everything. I was much more relaxed on stage."

At this point, my hand was flying, pen grasped in my fingers, as I tried to capture what Michael was saying in my journal. I silently thanked God that I'd remembered to set up my laptop next to me, recording our conversation.

"It's like, you have a gift. When you have a gift, it's your job to give it to people. When you look at what you have as a gift and an opportunity to give, it relaxes you. It puts you in a much better position because now your job is simply to give, not to get. So, no matter what you're doing, if you will ask yourself 'What can I give?' it will literally change *ev-er-y-thing*."

I finished scribbling my notes and grinned at the way Michael inflected the word "everything" by punching every syllable. *"Don't worry about what you get, just focus on what you give,"* I thought to myself. What a freeing idea, to not be responsible for manipulating people into giving me what I want, but only focusing on what I give to others.

How crazy would that be? If we were able to love someone without having to be loved in return? If we were able to give people opportunities even if we were never repaid for them? If we were able to get on stage and crack jokes or share a message regardless of whether we got laughs or got elected as camp president?

How crazy would that be, if we were able to give without having to get something in return? Because if that were possible, we could then give life everything we've got.

But that's impossible, right? I mean, we give what we have to in order to get something we want in return, and it's against logical self-interest to give more than that—right? It's psychologically impossible, right?

Yeah, tell Michael Jr. that. God sending his son Jesus to die for us didn't make logical sense, and we aren't logical beings. Living all out is impossible? No, we're on a clock to change the world—and as far as I can see, it's necessary.

Every once in a while, it seems we're reminded of how fleeting life is. For me, that week at camp with Anna was one of those times. As much as I wanted to sulk about the election loss, and as much as fear demanded I sit down and accept the way things were, I couldn't. I would never see this week again. And even though Anna and I had lost the election, we still had a ton of momentum—so what were we doing by giving up?

We only get to live high school once, this year once, this week once, this day once, this moment once, and this life once. As Roxanne Parks, an inspirational speaker for homeschooling mothers, would tell me, "Make the most of every moment you have, because you don't get to redo last Tuesday."

Killing it in life isn't about one grand achievement; it's about the way you live every single day. It's not about one success, but about creating significance in every would-be failure. It's about seizing every single moment you have, regardless of whether you may fail or get hurt—because ultimately, you don't get to decide how long you live, only how much you live.

What are we scared of? We're scared of getting laughed at, so we don't try what's not been tried before. But if you will be brave enough to absorb embarrassment at first, who's laughing when you eventually succeed?

We're scared of rejection, so we mutilate our personality and character to fit in with everyone else. But if you will be brave enough to be yourself and stand for what's right, you will strengthen the backbone of like-minded leaders so much so that they rally around you. And at that point, who cares about the jeering crowd?

We're scared of dying, so we play it safe and cautious. But here's what I want to know: For some reason, is God's love for us and strength to protect us more amplified in our living room than in the center of his calling?

The world cowers in their comfortable, safe lives, screaming at you to live cautiously so you can be like them and arrive at death with flawless skin—and a heart rotten from regret. But I don't see the point.

Author and speaker Rabbi Daniel Lapin reminded me during our interview, "Maximize every second you have in life, because the only commodity you'll ever truly run short of is time." And that's part of the truth so many of us are blind to. We're on a clock between birth and death, and all that matters is what happens between those two events. As far as I can see, there's no time for caution.

Limitless

You're too young to know. You're too young to matter. You're too young to change anything. You're too young to understand. You're too young to keep up. You're too young to help. You're too young to make a difference. You're too young to do it. You're too young.

That's what we're so often told growing up, and it seems that more often than not, in our teen years we eventually come to believe it. We buy the lie that the only point of youth is to have fun, get wasted, get high, and get laid as much as possible, and we can worry about all that "Does my life matter?" nonsense once we get old.

Maybe our teen years are where it all starts, because for the rest of our lives we seem to constantly be paralyzed by being "too" something. Too young. Too old. Too weak. Too dumb. Too early. Too late. Too scared.

I grew up hearing loud and clear from people that I was "too young," like most kids do, but my mother wouldn't let me believe it. Her words were softer than my shouting peers and society's booming voice, but Mom's voice was closer, right against my ear every night. She would say, "Holden, don't ever let anyone tell you that you're too young."

Back in 2016 when the call from Louisiana came in with Sadie Robertson—the *Duck Dynasty* gal—on the other end, I remember there was one question pressing against my mind. Here Sadie was, having written a book and embarking on a speaking tour—and for some reason, talking with me. Me! Some eighteen-year-old dude from Oklahoma with no name, no insane talent, no vast expanse of wealth, nothing. So of course, my question was why.

"Sadie, why do you do it all? Why do you push yourself? The writing, speaking, creating, leading—all of it. Heck, why are you talking with some teenager from Oklahoma when there are a hundred other things you could be doing right now?"

Her answer came swiftly. "Because when I was a little girl, I didn't know anyone who wasn't a Christian, so I prayed that God would send people my way who didn't know Him so I could share his love with them. And that's what he's done! He's given me this crazy platform and all this influence, and I know why: to use it to tell people about Jesus. And I don't want to miss out on that."

I knew exactly what she meant. It was the reason I was doing this bizarre interview project: I had once prayed to God for a second chance at meeting some rap star, and the answer to that prayer had changed my life.

But I wanted to challenge the idea a little bit and see how Sadie responded, so I countered, "That's awesome! But let me ask this: what about people who don't have that kind of crazy influence? What about young people who want to make a difference, but simply feel like they're too young or too under-qualified?"

I wasn't sure what to expect in response to that question. I mean, after all, she was Sadie Robertson. She was famous, talented, and had a TV show. Sure, easy for her to talk about making a difference, and good for her for doing so, but what about the rest of us at ground zero who aren't famous?

After thinking about it for a moment and then sharing some initial thoughts, Sadie brought her thoughts to a final point and said, "If you don't put a limit on what God can do through your life, there won't be one."

Those words echoed in my mind for weeks after, eventually driving home a truth to me that I now live by. It's a simple idea, really. Why don't small dreams spawn miracles? Because we dream small dreams with eyes closed, daring to think no bigger than the comfort of our beds, and it takes no miracle to stay asleep. We sit around, wondering why God doesn't open the gates of heaven and flood us with power and fame.

If God would just give us our own TV show, then we could make a difference, right? If God would just make us famous, then we'd have what it takes, right? If God would just put us up on stage, then we could change the world, right? Ha, bless our poor hearts and lazy, hazed-over, sleep-filled eyes.

Sadie didn't start off famous. When she had first prayed for God to send people her way who didn't know him, she had been no more than a little girl from Louisiana with a country accent, surrounded by a family who sold duck calls for a living.

She wasn't on a TV show, she wasn't born a celebrity, and she wasn't destined to be a music star, but she had a willing and passionate heart. And God can do more with that than he can with a mountain of solid gold. She started where she was with what she had, and as she continued to be faithful with little, God entrusted her with more—and eventually, a lot more.

God will work through you to the extent you're willing to pour yourself into others. Doug Carter, senior VP of EQUIP Leadership in the John Maxwell Company, told me, "Be an investor, not an adviser. Partnerships are only formed around investment. As with the boy who gave his two fish and five loaves of bread to Jesus so he could miraculously feed thousands, we too have to give God our effort and passion, not just give him advice. You have to give your lunch." Making a difference in the lives of others is simply a matter of how much you're willing to give toward life and people.

One of the greatest criticisms I ever got on my project of 500 interviews was "You just want to meet and interview people because they're famous!" No, that wasn't why. As a matter of fact, most of the people I interviewed weren't "famous." For those I interviewed who are famous, like Sadie, my interest wasn't in their fame as such but in why they were famous in the first place.

For Sadie, her fame cascades from her love, authenticity, and boiling passion. That's why people look up to her, and that's why I wanted to interview her. I know from my own experience that you'll never learn anything from merely famous people, but you will learn oceans' worth from passionate people. And it just so happens that passion can often make people famous.

Today, God continues to breathe through Sadie like a blacksmith inflating his fire with a pair of bellows. Yet, God doesn't choose Sadie because she's famous, but because she's awake and willing. That's the secret: to live limitlessly, simply be fervently willing—because when God is with you, the only limit that exists is the one you accept.

Wake Up

What are we doing down here? Playing it safe, risking as little as possible, living according to what skeptics see as realistic. Oh, but we're Christians, so let me rephrase that: we're "waiting on God's calling," when deep down we know his call has lingered since we were children. We're "content where we are," when really we know that being content and, on the other hand, going stagnant are as different as pearls and gravel. We're "just doing the safe thing," when in truth we know that faith is as unsafe as the raging sea.

And what great prayers do we pray? That the challenges and dangers around us shrink so we don't have to grow. That the opposition we face is weak so we don't have to get uncomfortable. That someone else dares to roar at the darkness and lead in our place so we can keep watching our numbing TV show.

We don't know what we're living for, so we guess it's for fortune, fame, and glory. Oh, but we're Christians and we phrase it differently, don't we? We're "living for God's glory," which is obvious because, well you know, we point our index finger up in the air sometimes.

I was once told by Nathan Knight, a church planter in DC, "Society is immune to the gospel. Like being injected with a vaccine, we've gotten just enough of it to not get it." And so we are. We're immune to the truth and blind to what's at stake.

We go to church and listen to sermons, we go to coffee shops and talk about "what Jesus is doing in our lives," we recite comments we've heard from our pastor, we go to Christian summer camps, we "bless" our food before eating it, and we put on an act when other Christians are around. We go through the motions like a surgeon operating on air. We look like we've got it all together, living the life we were born to live in full vibrancy—but if you take a closer look, you'll see we're just sleepwalking.

Come on, *wake up!* The only hope of life this world has burns inside us, yet we crawl deeper into the covers of our warm and comfortable bed. WAKE UP! Someday, we're going to get to the end of our life and realize we didn't really live any of it because we were always asleep.

What does it matter that God gives us vision if our eyes are never open? WAKE UP! We're sleeping life away, sinking deeper into the comfort of our dreary living rooms, secure jobs, perfect plans, familiar routines, and safe answers, lulling ourselves to sleep like a baby in a cradle.

The talents pulsating in your hands, feet, and mind like electricity were given to you for you to inspire the world with. The audacious dream weighing on your mind like a dumbbell was given to you because God knew you were the only one who could build it into reality. The drive burning inside you like gasoline in a race car was poured into you for so much more than the ambition to make yourself comfortable.

You've got one life to live. Don't waste it!

Wes Lane, the founder of SALLT who I've mentioned previously, once told me, "When I die, I want there to be a collective sigh of relief from hell." With that quote in mind, here's a question: Will the magnitude to which you live drive such an impact into the world that hell is shaken by it, or will evil be indifferent to the fact you ever existed?

Most people are sleeping their way to death. Are you?

Answer that question today, and tomorrow, and the day after that. And force yourself to open your eyes to your purpose every time you ask it—because to live life wide awake, you have to wake up every day.

Chapter 10

SUNRISE

"Ever since I was saved I cannot stop telling people about what Jesus has done for me and what he can do for them. It's shut up in my bones, I cannot help it. It's almost like Jesus has left me no other choice. It's do this or die."

—Christine Caine, activist,
author, speaker, interview #490

It was June of 2016 at about 4 p.m., and I was driving my Jeep down the highway on my way to a venue in Oklahoma City where Christine Caine would be holding an event that night. The sky was clear and the air was warm, with the sun basking the left side of my face and neck in yellow beams of sunlight.

It may sound strange, but I had dreamed of meeting Christine Caine since I was a boy. As an activist for social justice and against human trafficking, an author of bestselling books, an international speaker, and ultimately, as a worldwide leader and warrior of God's kingdom, Christine has always been a hero to me. And as if the fire obviously roaring inside her wasn't enough of a reason for me to look up to her, she also has an awesome Australian accent.

I'd prayed for the opportunity to talk with Christine since beginning the 500 interviews, but I eventually came to think it wasn't going to happen. After over a year of trying to connect with Christine's team and schedule a phone interview with her, I hadn't even received a hint that she would end up having time to talk with me. As the months rolled by and my number of interviews increased—as I got closer and closer to finishing all 500 them—I'd pretty much given up on connecting with her before the end of my project.

But then one day, as I was scrolling through Instagram, I ran across something that made me decide to try to connect with Christine one last time: she was going to be in Oklahoma City—just twenty minutes away from my house—the following month to speak. So I called Christine's office immediately and asked about meeting with Christine while she was here in Oklahoma. For the first time, I was told it might just work.

Sure enough, a couple weeks later, I had confirmed a half-hour meeting with Christine backstage before she spoke. I was stoked! I wasn't just getting to talk with Christine over the phone—I was meeting her in person in my home city!

Desperate

I've heard it said that the two most important days in your life are the day you're born and the day you find out why. For me, if there were ever such a day in my life, it was the day I met with Christine. It wasn't necessarily because of Christine or any one thing she said. My conversation with her was simply the tipping point for an accumulation of things that had been building up for me over the past two years, throughout my project, and ultimately throughout my life.

On that day, nearly everything I'd experienced and learned over the past two years finally culminated and came together. And I thank God it did, because it was at that time in my life that I felt more hopeless and empty than I'd ever felt before.

Leading up to the day I was scheduled to talk with Christine, I had been becoming increasingly panicked about my project and book.

I had started working on compiling my interviews into a book back at the beginning of the year and, with no idea what writing a book actually took, had set the goal of completing my first draft by the end of the summer of 2016.

But by late May, I started to realize that thinking I could have the first draft of my book done by the end of summer was ludicrous. My deadline was self-imposed, but I had shot my mouth off about it a little bit, so a large number of my friends and family's friends knew that the first draft of my book was supposedly going to be done by August. As people continued to ask me "how it was coming," I continued to feel more and more pressure to do something I now knew was nearly impossible.

After wrapping up a journey as monumental as I felt mine was, with the 500 interviews, I felt a ton of pressure to know *everything*. I was trying to write my book as if I had everything figured out in life—because, after all, I had just spent nearly the past two years learning from the most successful, passionate, and wise leaders I could find. Surely their cumulative wisdom should have become evident in me, right? I mean, that's at least what I thought everyone expected.

On the outside, I managed to keep up a pretty good image by the way I talked and acted, convincing people that I was high-rolling, on fire for Christ, and writing a book so chock-full of wisdom that it might surpass the book of Proverbs. But behind that image, I was falling to pieces.

I didn't have everything figured out, so everything I wrote in my manuscript felt flat, empty, and fake. I felt detached from it all, as if I were trying to tell another person's story.

And with each new word I wrote down, I felt like I was selling my soul and somehow compromising the truth and power of the journey I had actually gone on. Before long, I even started to question myself: *"Have I really learned anything at all? Or is everything I'm writing just stuff I'm making up in hopes that it sounds good?"*

It didn't help at all that with each new person who asked how my book was coming along—adding, of course, that they "couldn't wait to read it"—I felt increasingly obligated to write a book that I thought everyone would like. But what I had discovered is that it's impossible to create anything that everybody likes. In writing up my story and journey of interviews so as to make myself appear like the Christian golden-boy I thought everyone expected me to be, I found myself trying to be someone I knew I wasn't. And I hated it.

The more I thought about it, the more I realized I was right back where I'd been when I started the whole interview project: being who I thought people wanted me to be and doing what I thought would get people to like me, instead of being who I was made to be and doing what would rally people together. Something that was yet again driving me insane.

The old, familiar question that I'd struggled to answer so many times before had returned to me again, routinely shuddering through my thoughts like thunder across the sky: *"Why?"* Why had I really been doing all these interviews? Why was I writing this book? Why was all this worth it? At the moment, my focus was on why writing the book was worth it, but really, I was searching for an answer that encompassed a lot more than writing a book. *Why is life worth it?*

Fiercely desperate, I found myself constantly trying to answer the question, each time coming at it from a different direction. *"Why? To go on an adventure. So, why go on an adventure?"* At this point, I saw one immediate answer: *"Because adventure makes me feel alive."* But is that really all that life is? A mission to feel how you want to feel?

No. I loved feeling alive, but somehow, I knew good feelings were merely a byproduct of the real "why." So I pushed the answer further: *"I wanted to live an adventure in order to inspire people. Why? To make a difference. Why?"*

I didn't know. Because God had called me to. And why did I care what God said or thought? Because I wanted to get to heaven, to avoid going to hell, and to experience everything God had for me. To show his light to the world, to avoid spending life in sin and misery—whatever. I could give any reason I imagined, but when I asked *"Why that?"* the only answer I could come up with was the same: *"For some kind of feeling."*

No matter how hard and long I racked my brain to find an answer other than "to feel good," I couldn't. At the start of my project, the simple draw of earning a car, meeting cool people, going cool places, and being able to make a difference through my project had been able to draw me forward, but now I'd accomplished all that.

The deal made between Dad and I was that I got the car at the end of the interviews, and now I was ten interviews away from being done. I'd met cool people, I'd gone cool places, and I'd found the answers to more questions than I could ever count. Now, I was left empty. Besides, looking back now, I was forced to ask myself: Why had all that been worth it? Had it all really just been for a feeling?

Christine Caine would be my 490th interview, and in the few months leading up to that point, I'd worn myself out in regard to what I could get from writing the book. That's why I was ready to quit. My original answers to the "Why?" question had lost their luster and were no longer enough.

Realizing that maybe there was no greater answer to "why" than to feel good, I forced myself again, as I had many times before, to dream of being famous, of making a ton of money, and of discovering new opportunities as the result of my book. Anything that would make me feel good.

I was well aware of how prideful and self-absorbed all of the so-called "dreams" were that I was trying to force upon myself, but I didn't care. I desperately craved purpose like a starving person craves food. But if anything, those efforts only made me feel worse.

Some days I felt so fed up with writing, and with my project in general, that I considered setting my fourteen journals full of interview notes on fire and snapping my laptop in half. Why not? It would relieve me of all my stress, and the purpose of life was to feel good, right?

Looking back, I think the only thing that kept me from doing so, ironically, was stubborn pride—giving up was the weak way out, and I refused to be weak. Probably something I'd developed years ago while running suicide-sprints back in basketball practice. However, I'm certain that if I hadn't found something worth continuing to fight for, and fast, I would've soon given up completely.

Therapy

The Saturday before meeting with Christine, I found myself teetering so far on the edge of giving up that I allowed myself to unofficially quit for the weekend. For one, my mind needed the rest. And secondly, I knew that for every second more I allowed myself to labor over the laptop document containing my work-in-progress book, I ran a greater risk of a sudden meltdown in which I might delete the entire manuscript from my hard drive. I needed to spend the weekend recollecting some of my sanity.

I called a friend and mentor of mine, Lew Sterrett, whom I've mentioned before, and asked if he'd help me think through some stuff in regard to my interview project—and life in general. He said to come meet him at his ranch Monday morning. I was meeting with Christine on Monday night, so that worked for me.

Monday morning, I woke up early to get in a quick workout session before grabbing a Gatorade at the closest gas station to our house and hitting the road for Lew Sterrett's ranch an hour and a half away. When I got there, Lew took me on a quick tour of his ranch, since it was the first time I'd actually ever been there, and then we went to his rustic, mountain-themed office. I loved it—rugged-feeling places always helped me think.

Foregoing my attempts at maintaining composure, I let loose about the ugly mess inside me, no longer trying to hide the raw, jagged emotions locked up there. I no longer cared if people knew I was a mess. I was falling to pieces, my book felt fake and pathetic, I was freaking out—which is something I very seldom do—and I felt lost. Oh, I felt as lost as a shipwrecked blind man.

After I ended my rant, we just sat there in silence for a few moments while I caught my breath and Lew processed all I had told him. Then he said, "Holden, struggle is the sign of life. Having the guts to struggle in front of others is the sign of life inside of you. That's part of what it takes to be a leader." With that, he started asking me questions, helping me understand things, and showing me who I was when I myself couldn't see.

One of the questions I'd asked Lew was: "What does it all come back to? What's the point of all this?" His answer had been simple: "Love. It all comes back to love." A powerful idea, I thought, but the question persisted in my head all the same: *"Well, then why love? Is it just because love makes us feel good, or is there something greater?"*

I didn't know, but I didn't stress over it as I had previously. Despite the questions and frustration still swirling inside me, I left my "therapy session" with Lew experiencing a level of peace I hadn't felt in a while.

I won't soon forget the things Lew told me that day and the wisdom he shared with me. But the one thing I'll always remember is him caring enough and believing in me enough to simply invest his time and attention in me. That alone may have brought me more peace and strength than anything he said. He didn't have to meet with me, and he didn't owe me anything, but he spent all morning pouring into me simply because he cared about and believed in me. This was real love he was showing me, and something about it felt powerful beyond selfish desire. If only I knew what that was…

And that's where the story from earlier picks back up. I was only about ten minutes away from the venue where Christine Caine was speaking, the sun's warm beams of light pouring in through my open window, when exhaustion suddenly hit me like a semi-truck. Emotionally drained from the mess I was wrapped up in, I'd been running on hardly any sleep for the past couple weeks, and it had finally caught up with me. The road I was driving on began to blur so much that I began sticking my head out my Jeep window in hopes that the rushing wind would revive me and keep my eyes peeled open.

"This is not good," I thought to myself, head hanging limply like

a rag doll out the side window. *"I'm about to walk inside Crossings Church for an interview with Christine Caine, and I'm going to pass out in front of her."*

Then, I had an idea. I needed a big can of Red Bull, otherwise known as the drink of gods and the fountain of youth. I still had nearly an hour before I was supposed to meet with Christine, so I pulled into a gas station, snagged the first can of Red Bull I saw, paid for it, and immediately started downing the can right in front of the cashier. By the time I got back in my Jeep, I'd finished half the can. Then, with a huge gasp of air and sigh of relief, I shook my head and looked around.

My whole world seemed electrified.

Everything I've Got

Thirty minutes later I was backstage, anticipating Christine's arrival to the scene. Staff buzzed around and I was given little notice as I sat patiently, thinking to myself. Despite the Red Bull feeding me physical energy, my mind was still worn and emotions frayed. While usually, in the back of my head, there was the constant whisper of fear urging me to win people's admiration—and the resulting mental focus on how to get them to like me—fear was silent this time.

I'd spent so much time recently panicked over the progress of my book and trying to answer this stupid question of "why"—and on top of that, worrying about situations with friends and about what I was going to do after writing the book—that I didn't have the emotional capacity to be scared. I didn't have the mental strength to think up tactics and strategy for getting Christine to like me. All I had the strength to do was be me, so that's what I decided to do: I wouldn't even try to "get" Christine to like me. I would only focus on being myself and loving her.

Finally, Christine and her family arrived on the scene through the back door. I watched as they all greeted some of their backstage staff.

Then one of Christine's team members, Amanda-Paige, introduced me as the young man who was there to interview her.

Normally I greet people with, "Hey, Mr. or Mrs. So-and-so! I'm Holden, it's awesome to meet you!" followed by a firm handshake and excited grin. But before I could even get out the first word, Christine beat me to the greeting. She threw her arms wide to give me a hug, exclaiming in her charming Australian accent, "What's up, mate?"

I loosed a broad smile across my face, genuinely feasting on the warmth of Christine's welcome and overcome with a wave of happiness. In my edgy state, even something so small as Christine's greeting touched my heart.

After a brief moment of getting to know each other and comparing suntans, Christine took a seat so her makeup artist could get to work and I pulled up a chair next to her.

After sitting down, I took a deep breath. Not because I was nervous, but because I wanted to remember this moment. Dude, I was about to commence my interview with Christine Caine! I usually came to interviews equipped with a pre-crafted question, tailored specifically for the person I was interviewing and that I would ask to kick things off, but not this time. This time, there was only one question I could possibly ask, because it was the same question ravaging my mind like a bull in a china closet.

Steeled by Red Bull and trying not to use an Australian accent, I began, "Christine, I'm curious—"

She cut me off. "Yes, mate? Oh I want to know, am I the first person you've ever interviewed while they were having mascara makeup applied?"

I laughed hard and said, "Yes, you are! You're one of the most unique interviews I've ever had!" Then I asked my question, knowing I had rarely ever asked a question before with such an intense desire to know the answer: "Why do you do it all?"

I paused to see if I needed to explain the question further, but I didn't. Christine knew exactly what I was asking.

"Hmm, if I boiled it all down, since I was saved I cannot stop telling people about what Jesus has done for me and what he can do for them. It's shut up in my bones, I cannot help it. It's almost like Jesus has left me no other choice. It's do this or die.

"I've been going this fast, this passionate, this full of purpose for twenty-five years now. Jesus never called me and saved me to a safe and comfortable life. He called me—and you and all of us—to be dangerous to the kingdom of darkness. Passivity, safety, comfort—I never put those words together with being a Christian. Passivity would kill me. It's like, in this world I'm already dead. You can't kill me. Now let's take the Gospel into a lost world."

Thirty minutes later, Christine's makeup was done, and so was the time allotted for our conversation. She invited me to stay for the event that evening, we got a picture together documenting that I taught her how to do a Shaka (a.k.a. the "hang loose" hand sign), and then I turned to make my way out of backstage and into the auditorium that was currently filling up.

In that moment, my world shook, but gently. My eyes opened, but softly. It was as if after the long and cold night, the first glow of sunrise had just broken over the horizon. As I walked out from backstage, tears began to stream down my face.

For the first time, I finally saw why it was all worth it. Why life was worth it. Why love was worth it. Why the fight was worth it. For the first time, my soul resonated with a pure and ocean-powerful understanding that life was about more than just me.

That night, God instilled an idea in me that I'll never forget—a truth that I live by every single day, and one repeated throughout this book: *A life worth living isn't about getting all you can get, it's about giving it everything you've freaking got.*

Bring It

Why? Because I want to live an adventure. Why? For one, because that's how God made me, and secondly, because I want to inspire people. Why? Because I want to make a difference. Why? Because I want to inject the world with love and watch it spread across humanity like wildfire consuming a forest.

And why? *Because Christ first loved me* (1 John 4:19).

It's that simple. We love because Christ has so over-flooded us with love that we cannot do anything but overflow with it. It's who we are. Like Christine said, "It's shut up in my bones, I cannot help it."

Christine does all she does because there's something bigger than a desire for safety and comfort driving her. For all God has done for her, the only response she's capable of making is to take that same love, life, and light that she's been filled with and bring it to others. That's the same point I eventually reached after talking with her, except for me it took eighteen years of grinding through life, failing, getting ticked off, breaking down my pride, and soul searching to finally reach it.

Out in the auditorium after talking with Christine, I remembered back to the time this whole obsession had begun: the time I'd met Lecrae, the Christian rap star. As you'll recall, I'd screwed up my first chance to talk with him, prayed for a second chance, and God had given me that second chance—something I didn't take lightly. Having grown up longing to know what it meant to "truly live," I had dedicated myself and the 500 interviews project to finding out.

Over the many months and hundreds of interviews that had followed, my obsession with answering that question had only intensified. At times, it had threatened to drive me insane. Other times, it had fueled me with strength and passion. But no matter what, it had always been there.

Now, in finally catching a glimpse of the truth behind my question, my obsession didn't relax. Instead, it refocused and intensified. A year and a half ago when God gave me that second chance at talking with Lecrae, I'd been right: it was for something far greater than my own ego and a vehicle. But what I now realized was that everything I'd done and been given was also for something far greater than just finding the truth and hope behind my boyhood question—it was so that once I did find that truth and hope, I could bring it to others.

That night, I also finally understood the truth behind the first thing Lecrae had told me, his greatest word of wisdom to young people like me: "Everyone has gifts and talents, and if you find those they'll take you places. But to find your purpose, you first have to find God." I had never really understood the second part of that statement about "finding your purpose in God." That is, until now.

The gifts and talents each of us have will take us places if we know how to use them, but the only ones who will go as far as they can possibly go are the ones whose "why" lies in something greater than themselves—in God. That's why Lecrae had taken the time to talk with me. We'd been on different levels, me being a kitchen boy and him a rap star, but the call on our gifts and talents was the same: use them to love others.

To truly live, you have to do more than just catch fire with the spark God's given you—you have to *bring it*. You have to bring fuel to those who are burning. Bring warmth to those who are lost and hurting. And bring fire to the blackest shadows. To truly live, you have to reach the breaking point where you're no longer going as far as you need to in order to get something for yourself, but going as far as you possibly can to bring the light of life to other people.

Something I remember Mark Batterson told me was: "My dream for my kids is not that they don't do anything wrong. I mean that's great, but that's breaking even, and according to the parable of the talents, breaking even is basically breaking bad. That's not good enough. God wants more of a return than that. He wants us to risk being our best."

God wants more of a return than good enough. Lukewarm, breaking even, getting by—that doesn't cut it for God, and it doesn't cut it if you want to live to the maximum of what life can be.

With all my heart, I believe God doesn't simply demand enough. Rather, he demands *everything*, as does a life worth living. If all you spend your life doing is accumulating as much stuff as you can, you'll get to the end of life only to wonder how it ended up so empty. Life to the fullest isn't something you get from the world; it's something you pour into the world from inside yourself. Like the rising sun, the spark God gives us is not ours to contain, but to use to light up the darkness.

Children of Light

So perhaps you're wondering, *"You told me just earlier that you weren't capable of finishing writing your book, but here I am reading it—so what happened?"* Right. This is what happened.

After talking with Christine, participating in the pre-worship session for the event, and listening to Christine speak for a little bit, the thoughts whirling in my mind forced me to leave. I needed some space and quiet to think. Finally noticing how hungry I was from not having eaten since that morning, I got in my Jeep and drove to Tucker's Onion Burgers—one of my favorite burger places—which happened to be nearby.

As I worked on my burger and fries, I allowed myself to process the events of the evening and everything I'd learned. I now had a new understanding of why life and the fight for it were worthwhile. But even now, did I care enough to finish my book?

There were other ways to fulfill my newfound ambition for making my life matter that didn't require re-engaging that mess of words and attempts to meet expectations I had so far called "my book." I continued to eat and think, and with each new bite of onion cheeseburger, the load on my mind became lighter—until I eventually realized something.

If I let my fear and flesh win, that would be the end of it all. This passionate, adventure-filled journey I was on would be over. I would have spent two years of high school accomplishing a really cool project, and then I'd be looking for what was next. I would be lost again. Everything I talked about, and believed so strongly in, about adventure, dreams, passion, and catching fire was fake. How cheesy and pathetic those words would soon sound to me.

I would cross the finish line of a cool project, and would probably end up going on to Oklahoma State University or YWAM, simply because that's what I'd seen a lot of people do before me. Then I would spend the next few years there trying to figure out what I wanted to do with my life. I would eventually graduate, having discovered a skill that I'm good at and enjoy and that I can use to make money, but not something to which I truly feel called. I would be destined to simply remember back to the time I had once dared to follow my heart.

Ultimately, I would forever know that I'd left my calling abandoned on the side of the road—years ago back in high school when I had known God had raised me to be a warrior and wanted to use me, but I'd gone soft and given up. What a waste.

Prior to that night talking with Christine, a thought chain like this wouldn't have meant much to me. I was tired, scared, and done. What did I care if I didn't seize the potential I had to make a difference? Life was just about making myself feel good.

But now I knew life wasn't all about me, and that changed everything. Plus, there was newfound strength in the Tucker's onion cheeseburger I was eating. Now, filled with the strength of will to finally grasp it, I burned with one absolute commitment: God had given me this story, this opportunity, this journey, and I refused to waste any of it.

At that point and from then on, my book was no longer about what I could get from it. The stuff I could imagine myself getting from the completion of the book didn't draw me strongly enough. Now, the "why" that kept me pressing forward to write the book was that I decided to give *everything* for the love I had for Christ and others, which went far beyond what I would ever do to get something for myself.

What I've come to find is that when God sets you on fire, you'll live a life so insanely passionate, powerful, warm, and full of adventure beyond what you ever could live on your own. But be warned, because the natural side effect of burning with a fire bigger than you is that life is no longer just about you. Living for something bigger than yourself doesn't mean throwing your personal dreams, gifts, and passions out the window—no, just the opposite. It means blowing the flames of your dreams, gifts, and passions so bright and hot that they don't just serve you, but also illuminate and warm the world.

Just as when a river overflows a dam, which must eventually break and let the river loose, so also when God fills you with fire, the inevitable result is that you set others on fire. As the prophet Jeremiah once wrote, "If I say 'I will not mention him, or speak any more in his name,' there is in my heart as it were a burning fire shut up in my bones, and I am weary of holding it in, and I cannot" (Jeremiah 20:9). Truly, our God is the light of life, and if his spirit burns inside us, how could we possibly contain it?

When God fills you with his strength, passion, hope, and love, the inevitable result is that you flood others with those things—and if you don't let those things flow through you, they will drain out of you. Just as a pond clings to what it has and eventually dries up, while the river flows freely and grows bigger and stronger, so the vitality of the fire inside us hinges on whether we cling to it or let it grow beyond us.

Dreams and passion are meant to catch fire in others, hope is meant to be shared with others, and love is meant to touch others.

A friend of my dad and I's, Matt Myers, who is the co-founder of the leadership company GiANT, once told me, "You can tell the quality of a leader by looking at his followers." The same is true for our souls: you can tell the intensity of passion and love in someone by whether the fire has caught in those around them. If a fire doesn't spread, it smolders and dies.

So in the end, why? Why do we live? Why do we fight? Why do we love? Because we are children of light, and how can we do anything other than shine like the sun.

Chapter 11

LET'S GO

"I don't have any directions for you. I just want to get to know you!"

—Bob Goff,
author of *Love Does*, interview #200

"Boys, let's go!"

My three adventure buddies and I had just finished loading our four-wheelers on a trailer and strapping them down. After a proud moment of eyeing our work, I had clapped my hands and made the announcement. Time to move.

"Shotgun!" Brendan yelled, breaking into a sprint for the passenger side door of my family's pickup.

After we were all packed inside, I started the ignition and pulled out. It was 8:30 in the morning, and we were on our way to the sand dunes of Little Sahara Desert, Oklahoma. Blasting music, we spent the hour-long road trip planning ideas for the day.

"Anyone want a Red Bull?" Grant asked everyone as we finally pulled into the sandy nature park and I turned off the engine.

"Yeah!" came the unanimous answer, "I'll take one—hit me up—thanks man!" We all spoke at once, trampling over each other's words. Ian was in the back with Grant, so he got his first.

After a quick Red Bull toast, we unloaded the four-wheelers, packed our backpacks with camera gear, and strapped a wakeboard and tow rope down to one of the four-wheelers. We'd brought the wakeboard and tow rope to test an idea we had: tie the rope behind a four-wheeler, grab hold of it, and ride the wakeboard on sand like you would behind a boat.

We didn't know if it would work, but we were going to find out. After loading ourselves down with everything we needed, we grabbed our helmets and took off into the vast expanse of rolling sand dunes. Days like this one, beneath the blue sky with the wind blowing in my face, one hand holding a Red Bull and the other gunning the gas of my four-wheeler, were the best—but not because of where I was or what I was doing, but because of who I was with.

As kids, Brendan and I hated each other, Grant and I never saw each other, and Ian and I thought each other were weird. But as we grew older, we were slowly forced to trust each other more and more until eventually, we became a rascal band of brothers.

Justin Wren, the UFC fighter and missionary, once shared with me an African proverb that says, "If you want to go fast, go alone. If you want to go far, go together." As boys, the four of us hadn't known the proverb, but we had sure lived it. We relied on each other, stood up for each other, dreamed together, failed together, and trusted each other. As far as we were concerned, though life was easier and more convenient alone, it was far more powerful and fun together.

No One

Several weeks after my friends and I took our trip to the sand dunes, I was hovered over a workbench. Grasping a hand saw in my left hand, I cut and shaped a six-foot wooden plank held steady by my right hand and knee that I intended to build into a sand board—the equivalent of a snowboard, except that it would be used on sand dunes. After our trip to the Little Sahara Desert, we had found out wakeboards don't slide well on sand, and I was now working on a board I thought I could get to slide easier. I was already covered in sawdust head to foot, and with each new thrust of my saw, I sent even more billows of it into the air.

Suddenly, I felt my phone ringing in my left side pocket. "*Right when I'm in the middle of doing something. Typical,*" I joked to myself. I placed the saw down and pulled my phone from my right side pocket, spitting sawdust from my mouth as I did so. A friend of mine, about 10 years older than me, was calling.

Weird. I stuck my gloved left hand under my right armpit, squeezed it tight between my arm and ribcage so I could pull my hand free of the glove, and answered the call.

"Hey Kent, what's up?" I said, annoyed at the fuzzy taste of sawdust lingering in my mouth.

"Hey Holden!" Kent said excitedly. "Remember last week when we talked about how I'm hosting Bob Goff for a few days while he's here in Oklahoma, and you wanted to meet him?"

The question sent my memory reeling. *Duh!* Bob Goff, the *New York Times* bestselling author, lifetime adventurer, and one of my heroes in life was in Oklahoma right now. Kent had told me last week that since he was hosting Bob on his stay here, he might be able to find a time when I could meet Bob face to face.

"Yes! I remember!" I blurted into the phone.

"Well, can you get downtown in the next thirty minutes? Bob is doing an interview here and you might be able to meet him for a few minutes if you're here after it's done."

"I'll leave right now!" I exclaimed.

"Sweet! I'll send you the address. See you here soon!" Kent ended the call.

In a scramble, I threw all my tools on the workbench, grabbed my keys, and set down my work-in-progress sand board.

On the drive to Oklahoma City, I found myself recalling everything that had led up to this moment. When I had started the 500 interviews one year earlier, I'd suddenly had a ton of empty road time, so I had started filling that time by listening to audiobooks. The first one I had listened to was *How to Win Friends and Influence People* by Dale Carnegie, and the second had been Bob Goff's book *Love Does: Discover a Secretly Incredible Life in an Ordinary World.* That's when Bob had become a hero to me.

Somehow, Bob lived an adventure bigger and broader than the narrow energy drink and extreme sports niche with which I'd become familiar. Sure, he'd crossed the Pacific Ocean from California to Hawaii in a sailboat and done countless other crazy awesome stuff, but that's not what I'm talking about. He'd made getting into law school an adventure. He'd made his neighborhood into an adventure. He'd made raising his kids an adventure. I didn't know how he made such an adventure of the normal things in life, but I wanted to know.

I had always wanted to include Bob in my interviews project, but as far as I'd been concerned, he was a big important person and I would probably need to build up a really good résumé of interviews with other equally well-known people before his press team would consider me worth his time. So, that had been my plan for the first ten months of my project—until one day I learned Bob's personal cell phone number had been printed in the back of his book all along.

I guess it would have been more "professional" to have reached out to Bob's secretary and tried to set up an interview formally, but straight up calling Bob had seemed like more fun to me. Plus, I'd figured that's the way Bob would have done it if he were in my shoes, so that's what I had decided to do.

So much for waiting until I had an impressive résumé. I'd punched his number into my phone, and after a couple rings, an excited voice had answered the phone with, "This is Bob!"

"Hey, Mr. Goff! My name's Holden Hill. I've read your book and—"

"Hey, Holden! That's awesome! Did you like it?" He'd interrupted me and I'd laughed, relaxed a little by how relatable he was.

"Yeah, I loved it! I wanted to see if you had just a minute so I could share with you a project I'm working on."

"I've got one minute but not two, so we'll have to make it fast."

And so I'd given my spiel. I was on a mission to interview 500 Christ-driven leaders and was hoping to have 15 minutes to include him in the process.

After a few questions about my project, Bob had said he'd love to talk with me and would try to make it happen, and to email him about it so he could connect me with his assistant to help set it up.

Despite my initial hopes that Bob and I might have a phone call interview, his assistant had ended up having to tell me otherwise—that due to Bob's crazy schedule, he didn't have the time. However, at my request, she had agreed to let me send in some email questions.

I'd been disappointed but had understood perfectly. Bob had been insanely busy with speaking all over the country and trying to finish a new book he was working on, and on top of those two things, he also shouldered a thousand tons of popular demand from people asking him to participate in different events and opportunities. Then there had been me, some seventeen-year-old kid from Oklahoma working on something most people saw as little more than a school project. I'd been no one, and honestly, I'd considered myself lucky even to be allowed an email interview.

But then things changed.

Adventure of Love

"You have arrived at your destination."

The sound of my iPhone's GPS cut off my train of thought. I was here. I parked my Jeep, grabbed my phone, and ran inside the hotel. It wasn't hard to locate Bob, as there was an entire film set arranged on the right side of the hotel lobby. I immediately noticed my friend Kent on the other side of the set and knocked two fingers against my forehead in a slight salute. But I didn't want to disturb everyone by walking around to him, so I stayed on my side of the lights and cameras.

After a minute of watching the interview between Bob and the young female interviewer, I struck up a conversation with the guy standing next to me. Apparently, everyone there was part of a media team from a church in Tulsa, Oklahoma, and they were filming this interview to show during a sermon series they were doing.

As I watched and listened to the interview between Bob and the young woman, I became fascinated. Bob was just now telling a story of his I hadn't heard yet:

A few days earlier, he had left his vehicle in a parking garage and had returned to find every window busted and the contents of the vehicle stolen, which had included his laptop on which his new pre-published book was almost finished. It was gone now, all 60,000 words of it. Yet here Bob was, as joyful and whimsical as ever.

The story sent me thinking back again to my own experience with Bob six months earlier. As requested, I had sent my interview questions over email to Bob's assistant for her to get in front of him, and within a few weeks time, I had heard back—but not with the answers to my questions. No, this had been far better news: Bob had arranged for us to talk live over the phone!

A couple weeks later, when my phone had finally buzzed with Bob's number on the caller ID, one incessant question had pulsed through my mind: *"Why is Bob talking with me?"* It made all the sense in the world for him to divert his time elsewhere. I understood perfectly and would have done the same thing myself. But despite the fact I'd had nothing to offer Bob in return, he had made the intentional effort of setting aside fifteen minutes for me. Stunned by the surreality of the situation, I'd answered the phone.

"Well, Mr. Goff," I'd said after a minute of us getting to know each other better, "did you get the list of questions I emailed in?" The first question I'd wanted to ask Bob was on that list of questions I'd emailed his assistant, so I'd figured it was a good lead into our conversation. Little had I known he was about to answer the far deeper question I'd asked myself just before answering the phone.

"Yes, I did! But I honestly don't like answering questions like that. It just feels like homework to me. Holden, I want to get to *know* you!

"It's like if you're driving down the road and pull off at a quick stop to ask someone for directions. And that's what you're wanting from me: directions for life. And the thing is, the directions they give you will be valuable, but what if you also wanted to get to know them? How crazy would that be! If you just told the cashier, 'I want to get to know you'?

"That's why I'm talking with you right now, Holden, and that's why I put my number in the back of my book." Bob had paused then, and I'd remained silent as I'd scribbled notes in my journal. After a moment, he'd resumed.

"Holden, the real value of this project you're doing is in the relationships you're building with people, and even more so in keeping those relationships. Remember that the friendships you build with people will always be more valuable than the directions they give you."

Fast-forward six months and those words had stuck with me, now branded on the forefront of my mind today as I stood in the hotel lobby watching Bob being interviewed. Before long, the interview between Bob and the young woman ended and everyone started taking the set and equipment down. I stood aside and let the church's media team have the first conversations with Bob. After all, if it weren't for them, I wouldn't even be here.

Then, it was my turn. Cracking a broad smile, I approached Bob saying, "Mr. Goff! It's Holden Hill. I interviewed you last June. Kent told me you were going to be here and I wanted to come say hey!"

Bob laughed and said, "Hey, Holden! Call me Bob!" I was about to offer my hand to shake his, but then he threw his arms wide and beat me to the handshake with a big bear hug. You would never guess that this was the same man who just days earlier had his nearly finished, 60,000-word book manuscript stolen from him.

My book is roughly 60,000 words as well, and considering how much work I've put into it, it's worth more to me than everything else

I own put together—no exaggeration. But here Bob was, laughing and on the move, as vigorous and passionate as ever.

Eventually, we had to split. Bob went to get ready for his speaking event that evening, and I headed back to my woodwork project. Sending sawdust wafting into the air again as I cut back and forth on the plank, I allowed myself to think about the experience I'd just had.

Bob's an adventurer, just as I want to be. We both love daring ventures and ideas, pushing ourselves, and experiencing the wonder and beauty of the world. But the more I thought about it, the more I realized that all of that wild activity wasn't the real source of adventure. No, the real and greatest source of adventure isn't doing crazy stuff; it's having crazy love.

Bond

Binge-eating Chick-Fil-A waffle fries, with my earbuds in and listening to EDM music, I watched the time on my phone in anticipation. By a stroke of "luck," I had recently done a phone interview with a man from Oregon named Steve Ridgway. When at the end of our conversation I'd asked Steve if there was anyone he could connect me with whom would be worth including in my project, Steve had paused for a moment and then said, "Do you know who Jefferson Bethke is?"

For a moment, I had blanked on who this "Jefferson" was and had answered back casually, "No. Is he worth talking to?"

Steve had sounded shocked that I hadn't heard of Jefferson before and exclaimed, "Absolutely! He's a YouTuber and author from Maui, Hawaii. When we get off the phone, you need to look him up. I'm a friend of his and if you want, I can connect you with him."

I still hadn't been sure who this guy was, but had taken Mr. Ridgway's word for it and said, "Yes! I'd love to talk with him!"

As soon as Steve and I had ended our call, I'd looked Jeff up on YouTube. Wow, had I suddenly felt stupid. The moment I'd seen Jeff's face I'd instantly remembered who he was: I had just discovered this dude a few weeks earlier when my pastor, Craig Groeschel, had posted a picture with him on Instagram. After watching Jeff's viral YouTube video featuring his spoken-word poem *Why I Hate Religion but Love Jesus*—from which he has now taken the message and forged it into a book, titled *Jesus > Religion*—I had committed to eventually trying to earn an interview with him.

Now, several weeks later, sitting in Chick-Fil-A, I was scheduled to call Jeff at 1 p.m. my time, 7 a.m. Hawaii time. I was nervous, and the fact I'd been in a mess of drama with a friend of mine recently didn't help much. I tried to let the EDM music pounding through my earbuds drown out my concerns and bring my focus to bear on the moment, but it only partially worked. Half my attention was still on the collapsing friendship I was currently dealing with.

Finally, the time on my phone changed—1:00. I let the song I was listening to finish to the drop, dumped the rest of the waffle fries in my mouth, and chomped down dramatically in rhythm with the music. Here we go. I went to Jeff's contact and hit 'call.'

"Hey, man! What's up!" came Jeff's voice as he answered the phone, sounding down to earth and pragmatic. With that, we were off.

For the majority of our conversation, I kept my questions general and objective, but after thirty minutes of talking, I could no longer ignore the issue weighing on the back of my mind. I was dealing with one of the toughest friendship problems I'd ever faced, and here I was talking to one of the most influential voices in the world on relationships. I needed advice for right where I was, not just life.

I don't remember the exact question I asked right then, but I'll always remember what Jeff told me in response: "Holden, we're called to covenant with people, not contract. Real relationship happens when you could have left—but didn't."

Eventually, Jeff and I ended our call, and after wrapping my journal up in its leather strap and stuffing it in my backpack, I sat back in my chair and thought.

The issue on my mind was that recently, a close friend of mine had gone behind my back, broken my trust, and hurt me badly. I'd known that I'd merely been caught in the collateral damage of them fighting through some personal problems, but at the time, I couldn't have cared less. Also, the fact that they still continued to trash me behind my back and give me snide remarks didn't help much.

I was hurt and pissed off, and the forgiveness I had tried to maintain over the past few weeks was slipping. I wanted to lash back.

In fact, I had already started retaliating with my words whenever I got a snide remark or cold shoulder from them. I wanted to tear their reputation apart and wreck their life until we were even. I knew I could, and boy did revenge sound sweet.

That's where I now found myself, sitting in Chick-Fil-A after my phone call with Jeff. *"We're called to covenant with people... not contract. Real relationship happens when you could have left... but didn't..."* I repeated the statement to myself and let the words echo in my mind, rolling them around with my thoughts like fruit in my mouth.

As far as I could tell, Jeff had meant "contract" as a friendship built purely on what you could get from someone. I hated friendships like that. People would claim to care about each other and be friends, enjoying the increased popularity, cooler toys, and temporary pleasure that came as a result. But when the struggle of being friends became no longer worth the immediate payoff, they would be faced with a choice: Do I drop my friend and leave them now that the contract has expired, or am I actually in this friendship for the person and not just the benefits I can get from them?

That was the choice now staring me in the face, but I revolted against it. My friend's spite toward me had broken the contract between us, and now all I wanted to do was leave my friend hurting on the side of the road like they had tried to leave me.

"I'm not in this just for myself. Behind all the garbage my friend is dealing with, they truly are the kind of person I want to be friends with. It's just that there's no way I can possibly love someone who treats me like this," I told myself, trying to justify my attitude.

But then, plunging into my turbulent thoughts like a stone into a river, one annoying, stupid idea entered my mind that refused to leave: "*Forgive.*"

"*No! What kind of wuss doesn't hit back when someone hits them?*" I thought. I knew I could, and even *should* forgive my friend a few times as I'd already done, but how could I possibly forgive limitlessly? I couldn't, obviously. The draw I felt toward forgiveness was as absurd as climbing out of a ship to try walking on water. Spite and anger were my floating fortress, and without them, I would definitely drown.

Besides, showing love and forgiveness to my friend hadn't accomplished anything before, and that wasn't likely to change. If I tried showing any kindness to them now, they would probably just think I was mocking them, or at the very least, that I was being fake. How would forgiveness ever do any good?

Despite my resistance, though, the draw I felt toward forgiveness only intensified. It answered my excuses with the truth that I'd been forgiven of far worse than what I was currently struggling to forgive my friend for. And eventually, finding myself entertaining the idea that walking on water might just be possible, I made my decision: I didn't know how I would continue to forgive, and I didn't know how it would do any good even if I could, but I did know that I had to try.

In the following weeks, I stopped retaliating. I stopped fighting. I started letting go of my venomous thoughts. And though it took longer than the other changes, I even started trying to once again show kindness to my friend—not because I needed them to like me back, but because I saw that they needed it.

At first, as I had suspected, my friend took my change in behavior as me mocking them, setting them up, trying to fool them, or being fake. But that was alright. Getting them to feel forgiven wasn't the point. The point was for me to do what I could do by relinquishing my bitterness and let God take care of the rest—and take care of it he did.

As I started letting go of my fortress made of spite and anger, taking the attacks at me without retaliation, the craziest thing happened: I started to walk right over top of them. In fact, I soon became nearly invincible to the offensive behavior and derogatory comments I'd once been scared of being vulnerable to. Because, as I found out, when you truly learn to forgive, no attack or amount of malice can ever drag you under its surface. And in time, as I learned to live in forgiveness, my friend's wounds and pain healed along with the bond of our friendship.

Anthony O'Neal, a personality on the Dave Ramsey Show and part of the Ramsey speaking team, told me during our interview, "Don't build a relationship with someone for where they can take you, or for what you can get from them, but for who they are." I didn't fully understand what Anthony meant when he first told me that, but I do now.

Contracts are agreements made based on what people can get from each other, while covenants—*true* relationships—are commitments made based on what or who people can become together: unbreakable partners, brothers and sisters who know you as well as you know yourself, a team that trusts each other with their lives, or family by blood or bond.

Something my dad has always taught is that who you're becoming in life is far more important and powerful than whatever stuff you're accumulating, and that the relationships you build with people will determine who you become.

That's why I've learned that sometimes, you have to look past the glitter and gold, or past the dirt and pain as it may be, and see the person. Because the raw power and joy of relationships aren't in a contract written on paper, saying you can get a certain amount of stuff from someone, but in a bond of love and adventure you build together.

All In or Nothing

Last summer, some friends of mine and I had made plans to go to the Oklahoma City Fair after church one weekend. I had just asked my mom about it and gotten the thumbs up when my younger brother Brayden, eleven at the time, approached me and asked if he could go with me to church to meet up with his friend Stephen. I guess he'd overheard Mom and me.

I didn't mind and told him "sure," figuring Brayden could simply get a ride home with Stephen's family who lived just a mile from our house. But then, he asked if I could also take him to the fair with me after church.

"No," was my abrupt response.

Brayden wasn't satisfied with that and kept persisting, so I explained the situation to him. If any of his friends were going to be going to the fair, then I'd have no problem bringing him, but they weren't—it was only me and my friends going, we were older, and he just needed to go home after church. Brayden still wanted to go with me even after that, but I told him no again. I figured my friends might be annoyed by me bringing my little brother, and also, I didn't want to have to watch him the whole time we were at the fair.

For some reason though, leaving Brayden behind didn't feel right, and the closer the time came to leave my house, the more leaving him behind bothered me.

Finally, just before leaving my house, as I was wetting my hair and washing my face, a question crossed my mind: *"What kind of person do I want to be?"* Maybe the question sounds weird to you, maybe it doesn't, but it made me stop and think.

Then, after thinking for a moment, a second question compounded the one before it: *"In this situation, what would that kind of person do?"* I knew the answer to that.

I had just gotten in my Jeep, and Brayden was climbing solemnly in the passenger side to go to church with me, when I told him, "Hey, you can come to the fair. You're gonna be the only one your age, but heck, that's fine. Let's go."

He lit up excitedly. I had grabbed my longboard before getting in the Jeep in case I found somewhere cool to ride it at the fair, so Brayden ran and grabbed his, threw it in the backseat, and jumped back in the Jeep. Without a shadow of doubt, I knew that the kind of brother I wanted to be, the kind of *person* I wanted to be, wouldn't leave people behind for mere convenience—even if it was his younger brother.

As I continued to think about how the evening would play out, I became more and more confident that my friends would likely be entirely fine with seeing Brayden there. However, after telling Brayden he could come with me, I no longer even really cared how my friends took it. Whether they liked seeing Brayden there or not, my brother was more important to me than others' opinions.

After church was over, Brayden hooked up with his friend Stephen and decided that he didn't want to go to the fair because he wanted to hang out with Stephen instead. For a moment, I argued with myself about inviting Stephen as well so Brayden could still join me. Then, with a shrug of the shoulders, I said, "Stephen, you can come, too, if you want! I don't care!"

They discussed my proposal for a minute, but then decided they'd still rather just hang out at church and then go back to Stephen's house.

As I drove away from the church parking lot and hit I-35, surprisingly enough, I didn't find myself glad that Brayden and Stephen had remained at church. Instead, I found myself wishing that they had come. However, I also found myself without an ounce of regret, because I had given them the opportunity to come if they wanted to. I realized that day that the love I claim to have for God is realized by the love I show to others.

One of the other comments Jeff Osborne, the former prison inmate turned preacher from California I've mentioned previously, made during our interview was: "Love is never convenient, but it's always worth it."

I've come to learn for myself that following love means going out of your way. It means giving more and going farther than you have to. It means risking more than you would otherwise, and it means doing something you wouldn't do if your focus were only on you.

Real, raw, raging love only comes from who we are inside. Love can't be a charade to get people to love us back, to get people to like us, to get people to accept us, or to get anything else from people. It's like John 15:13 says, "Greater love has no one than this, that someone lay down his life for his friends."

And with that in mind, here's the truth: you won't take a bullet for yourself, but you'll take a bullet for someone you love. To truly love, you have to do so because you're filled with love, not because you're trying to get love in return.

It's all in or nothing. Love doesn't follow the path of comfort, security, and convenience, so you either chase love over everything else or abandon it. You either pursue those you love or abandon them. Love doesn't conform itself to the same path so many people conform themselves to out of fear and laziness. Love is always going to be out of the way, so you must simply decide: Do I value that which I want more or that which I love more?

In the end, perfect, raw, and overflowing love only comes from one place: my God who first loved and died for me. From what I've discovered, all of life comes back to love. If something's worth living for, it's also worth dying for, and all that's worth dying for is love.

I challenge you, if God's love burns inside you, just keep it simple and love full throttle. Love where it's dangerous, risky, and hard, and love like no one else dares to love. In the end, saying "I'm going" is more convenient, but saying "Let's go" is far more rewarding. And that's the way it is with love—because love is seldom convenient, but it's always worth it.

Chapter 12

FOR GENERATIONS

"I am not preparing my kids to die and go to heaven, but to live for Christ. We are here to LIVE for him, and if that means dying for him, so be it. But prepare to live, not wait to die."
—My dad, off the record

It was approaching twilight, with gray clouds covering the sky, and a group of roughly two dozen men stood in a circle around me. My dad was next to me. From above, the scene might have looked like the men of a small village gathered around a huge bonfire—except, instead of a fire in the middle, it was me and Dad.

I was fourteen years old at the time, and this was the culmination of a ceremony I'd long anticipated, a ceremony that my family and close family-friends carry out with their teenage sons to mark the first stage in our transition from boyhood to manhood. Since then, I've come to remember the event as my "manhood ceremony."

It's been different for every one of my friends. For me, my dad had brought together a group of over twenty men who were influential in my life. We were holding the ceremony outside, behind our house. I hadn't been informed of the evening's specific plan, but that was okay by me—it only intensified my excitement.

Each man there had pre-written a page or more of wisdom which they read aloud and then gave to me, and after that, I was asked to share a little from my heart on what all this meant to me. Now, Dad began speaking.

As the circle of men naturally formed around us, Dad came to the culmination of his speech. He turned aside and withdrew an unsharpened, but completely authentic broadsword I hadn't noticed so far from behind a rock, and then turned back to me to continue speaking, this time about the sword.

He reminded me that our great-, great-, however great-grandfather was Sir Andrew Moray, the Scottish companion-in-arms of Sir William Wallace. Then, after sharing with me what the sword symbolized, he handed it to me.

Steel blade, leather-wrapped handle, and plain steel pommel—altogether heavy enough that I had to grasp it in both hands to hold it adequately. Fittingly, it was a replica of William Wallace's sword from the movie *Braveheart.* I received it like I'd just been handed the nuclear football.

The sword now hangs against a wall in my bedroom, where I occasionally take it down to relish the feeling of it in my hands. I guess if I were the son of a knight 900 years ago and my father had given me a sword, its purpose as a weapon for good, against evil, and as a symbol of my family's legacy would have been served slung across my back every day. However, it's the 21st century, and so my sword serves its purpose in a different way.

The sword is a constant reminder to me that every day I wake up and leave my room, I carry a legacy—a vision—passed down to me from my father. For me, it's a symbol of the man my father has raised me to be, and that he believes in me. It is a constant reminder to me that though I don't carry the sword with me when I leave my room every day, I carry the responsibility of a warrior for Christ just as much as if I did: overcome evil with good, defend the weak, and stoke the battle cry of Christ to last for generations to come after me. Because in the end, if the fire inside me dies when I do, I have failed.

Ash

"I want to matter... because if I don't, what was the point of ever existing?"

That desire has saturated my life for as long as I can remember. Mine and everyone else's, I guess. We ravenously crave meaning, knowing deep down that just as ships weren't made to rust in the harbor, neither were we. We want to matter—no, we need to matter, because if we don't, we're as pointless as an equation with no solution. And for me, success was always my solution to the equation.

How do you matter? Work your tail off, take risks like you have a death wish, build an empire so magnificent that people look to you like a god? Get married in a London castle throne room, buy a mansion on the California coast and a 10,000 square-acre ranch in the mountains of Colorado? Appear as the leading role in a hundred blockbuster films and own a fleet of Lamborghinis, Ferraris, custom Jeeps, and souped-up pickups? Maybe own a few helicopters and a private jet, travel to and explore every amazing place there is on the planet, and die a legend?

That's how you matter, right? Because results matter—right?

I used to think so. But in November of 2014, just a few months after starting my interview project, I was no longer so sure. I had just walked out of my thirty-seventh interview wearing a thick brown-leather coat and even thicker socks, but thickest of all were my reoccurring thoughts of the past hour.

"Hello, ma'am! I'm Holden Hill. I'm here to see David Green this morning."

I had stammered the words an hour ago, partially because I was slightly nervous but mostly because I was extremely excited. I stood in the corporate headquarters of Hobby Lobby, the $3 billion dollar arts and crafts superstore chain. My meeting was with David Green, the seventy-three years old entrepreneur and founder of the company.

"Hi, Holden!" The front desk receptionist greeted me with a broad smile. "I'll let David know you're here! I'll need you to clip this on your shirt and wear it while you're here. It helps us keep track of guests and visitors."

She handed me a plastic tag with something printed on the front, and then somehow relayed the message to someone else that I had arrived. I wasn't really paying attention. Right then, I was still in a daze as the reality of the situation sunk in further and further.

I was barely beginning to scratch the surface of my project, and I was already meeting with David Green. David Green! A man I had heard legends about for years. The entrepreneur and now billionaire who had built Hobby Lobby from nothing. The man who donated fifty percent of his company's annual income to non-profit ministries every year. The man who had stood up against abortion by locking horns with the federal government, taking them to court in defiance of providing "The Morning After Pill" in his company's health insurance programs as was being mandated—and winning the case.

As far as I was concerned, he was the epitome of success. Surely if anyone had made their life matter, he had. After all, according to Forbes, he was the 234th richest man on the entire planet.

"Holden!"

The sound came from behind me, and I spun around. A man with a full head of white hair and an intricately designed purple dress shirt was walking toward me, a grin on his face. I'd never met Mr. Green before, but without a second thought, I knew this was him.

"Mr. Green! It's so awesome to meet you!" I exclaimed as I ran up to him and vigorously shook his hand.

"You, too!" Then, after I let his hand go, he asked, "Do you like coffee?"

I didn't, but I was trying to learn to, so I told him I did. With that, he clasped me on my left shoulder and escorted me down a hall to a small coffee bar, where he made each of us a cup. Then he escorted me to a boardroom where I was free to barrage him with questions about my core interest at the time: What did it take to be successful? And not the kind of short-lived success that it seems so many people scramble for. No, I didn't merely want to be successful while I was alive. I wanted to become such a success that I continued to matter even after I was gone. After all, success was what made people matter, right?

Eventually, after ten minutes or so of performing my interrogation, I needed a moment to think through my next question. I took a sip of coffee. Awful stuff. When I finally put the cup back down and looked back up at Mr. Green, he had a question for me this time.

"Holden, does Hobby Lobby matter?" he asked me, the tone of his voice now noticeably more intentional and serious.

Suddenly consumed with excited anticipation for what Mr. Green was going to say, and also confused at what he was really asking, I fumbled for my answer. After affirming to myself that Hobby Lobby was without a doubt one of the biggest successes in America, I stated what I considered obvious: "Yes, I think so…"

With a knowing grin, Mr. Green looked me in the eyes and shook his head. Then he said, "No, it doesn't matter, really. Given a hundred years, two hundred years, five hundred years, whatever it is, someday Hobby Lobby won't be around anymore. Eventually, all my success will die and return to dust just as I will.

"There are only two things that truly last: God's word and man's soul. The only thing that truly lasts and matters is the impact *I* have on *your* life and the lives of others for eternity."

As Mr. Green's words cut through my mind, my left hand and pen faltered over the top of my journal. My mind ran at a thousand miles an hour as I tried to process what he had just said. Mr. Green had just challenged one of my core perceptions of reality, saying that in the end, if all you ever do is succeed, then all you will leave behind is a big pile of ash. At first, I wanted to dismiss his words as nonsense. But for some reason, I couldn't.

As I walked out of the meeting, I ducked my chin into the fleece collar of my coat to protect myself against the biting cold air. I couldn't stop thinking about that one thing David had said. Success had always been my answer, but now, no matter how much I tried to return to my success-infused vision for life, it felt empty.

The unwanted question of it all was lodged in my memory like a piece of apple stuck between my teeth: *"If in the end success really does just turn to ash, then what never does?"*

Split Second

"Mom, why did you choose me instead of chasing your other dreams?"

I remember asking my mom the question one night several months ago when she came into my room and sat on the edge of my bed. I was up late working on my book and was just beginning on this very chapter.

Mom has homeschooled me and my four siblings our whole lives, but I know the stories well: the idea of homeschooling and my mom's life plans used to be as far apart from each other as the earth's north and south poles. By the sweat of her own brow, my mom put herself through college at the University of Oklahoma, earning a juris doctorate in law. Being highly ambitious and having come from a poor childhood, she was determined to make it big—so big that she *mattered.*

From her years in college and up to the day she gave birth to me, my mom was a hard-driving businesswoman and entrepreneur with dreams of big, roaring success. But then she had me, her first child, and I messed up everything. With her own all-in-or-not-at-all personality, my mom knew that she could either continue chasing her dreams of fame and fortune, or care for and raise me, but that she couldn't do both. And so she chose me.

That's where my question now sprung from: "Why did you choose me?" Not that I didn't already know the answer, but I guess that sometimes, we kids like to have the truth reinforced to us because that makes it feel all the more real. And plus, since I was beginning work on a new chapter, I was looking for inspiration.

My mom took my hand and told me again, as she had so many times before, "Because within a split second of looking into your eyes for the first time, I fell in love with you, and I knew in that moment that pouring my life into you and your siblings was more significant and lasting than anything else I could ever do. It was like, I guess I could have paid someone to care for you, but I could never have paid someone to love you."

I'd heard that answer many times, and never used to fully grasp what she meant—but this time, as I reflected on the question driving this chapter and on all I'd learned in regards to it, I finally understood.

In the months that had followed my interview with David Green, I had developed a heated search for the answer to my question, "What never turns to ash?" As crazy as it was, the more I started to look for answers, the more it seemed they were right in front of me.

One month after talking with David, I had an interview with Cary Summers—an entrepreneur, former executive with Bass Pro Shops and Abercrombie and Fitch, and currently the President of the Museum of the Bible in Washington, DC.

We'd been having a hearty conversation for quite some time when Cary's intercom buzzed. He picked up. I couldn't hear what was said by the person on the other end, presumably his assistant, but I did hear Cary say, "It's alright. Just keep him comfortable and tell him that I'll be out soon. I'm in an important meeting."

Suddenly, as Cary finished talking to the person on the other end of his intercom, a wave of alarm swept over me and I yanked my phone out of my pocket to glance at the time. Cary and I had scheduled our meeting for an hour, from 9 a.m. to 10 a.m., but now, it was after 11! As the realization of what had happened sunk in, I was shocked.

Cary, the president of one of the most prominent museums in the world, had been delaying his next meeting for over an hour in order to allow me, some sixteen-year-old kid with nothing more to offer than a sense of curiosity, to continue asking questions.

Stumbling to my feet, I blurted out an apology for having run so far past our allotted time. I was ready to leave. But Cary laughed and motioned for me to sit back down.

"Holden, don't worry about it! Our conversation right here is more important to me. I'll get to my next meeting soon enough."

Confusion flooded my face as I guiltily sat back down, completely at a loss for words. Cary saw my confusion and explained.

"Listen, let me explain something to you. We live for an instant on earth. An instant. And what I know is that the only thing that will last eternally after I'm gone is what I do to impact you and others for forever."

I absorbed what Cary said and relaxed a little bit, taken by surprise at how similar the statement was to what David Green had told me just a few months earlier. *"I wonder how many more times I'm going to hear this same thing,"* I thought to myself. As it turned out, from then on I never stopped hearing it.

Steve Trice, the founder and CEO of the multimillion-dollar company JASCO, and a man of massive generosity who I greatly look up to and who has been instrumental in my project, once summed up for me, "Someday, JASCO is gonna be all burned up. It's just temporary success that won't last forever. But so long as it does last, that temporary success is something God has entrusted to me to make an eternal impact on the souls of people."

Kirk Humphreys, a real estate entrepreneur and former mayor of Oklahoma City, told me, "At the end of the day, the only thing that remains is the impact you make on people."

Alex Kendrick, the award-winning actor, filmmaker, and director of the movies *Courageous*, *War Room*, *Facing the Giants*, and others, once shared with me, "All that will truly last after you die is your soul and the honor you gave to the Lord. So seek after eternal things and the purpose God has given you—not all this temporary fluff. For me, that purpose is telling stories to share truth that draws people to a closer walk with God."

Ross Hill, a mentor of mine and the CEO of Bank 2, which has consistently been ranked in the top five community banks of the entire United States, told me, "This temporary, fleeting success we have is merely an opportunity to influence people for the Lord. That—the difference you make in people's lives for eternity—is the only thing that really matters and truly lasts forever. My day starts with using my influence to talk with people and love them, and it ends with me sharing the gospel with them."

That's just a glimpse of the number of people who talked to me about this idea of "never ashes." Eventually, I came to understand it—but for some reason, no matter how much I wanted to, I could never fully believe it. For me, it was just an idea that I knew, but didn't own. But then that all changed.

As I write this, the three year anniversary of my project has just recently passed. This is real time. After I finish writing this chapter, I'm done. The last line of my past three years' project is inches away from me, and the mere prospect of crossing it is enough to send tremors of pleasure pulsing through my body. I've done it. I've beaten the odds. I've proven everyone who ever doubted me wrong. I've chiseled myself into a better, stronger man. I've finished writing the book I myself wasn't even sure I could finish. I've succeeded, and boy does it feel good.

My success matters, right? For a time, people are going to read this book I've written. People will care about my story, the mind and body I've developed for myself will thrive passionate and strong, and all of the success I've built will matter.

But no, the big secret hidden in front of my blind eyes is that it doesn't matter, right?

Someday, my book will fall into the past as it becomes too old-fashioned for anyone's taste. My story will be forgotten, my mind and body will grow ill and die, and all my success will eventually fade into oblivion just as waves on the sea eventually subside back into nothingness. It doesn't matter, right? Or does it? Which is it?

What matters?

I've spent the past three years searching for the answer to that question. Now, three years later, standing on the threshold of the very success I've sought after for so long, the truth has finally become real to me. Success neither matters nor doesn't matter. It's a tool, a weapon, a voice—and just like your voice, it's not the success that in and of itself really matters, but the impact you have on people with and through it.

We have a split second called "life" to make an impact that lasts forever. In our desperate search for meaning, we go wild to get everything we possibly can from the world, but fail to realize that what we get from the world for ourselves will die with us. The monuments we build in our name will crumble away as they're buried in the sands of time, and the fame we acquire will eventually fade into indifference. In the end, all that lasts is that which we pour into the world from inside ourselves, and especially what we pour into our kids and the next generation.

Gambler

There was a time when I wanted to make everyone think that this entire project, from the interviews to writing the book, was born from me, but the truth is that it's not. I was the one who made it all happen, but the ability to make it happen was born out of the wisdom of 500 leaders, the support of another 500-plus friends and family, the undying love of my six immediate family members, and one of those family members in particular: my dad.

Why does a boy's father charge his son with interviewing 500 impactful leaders? Why does he consistently stay up until 2 a.m. talking with his son to console him or give him guidance? Why does he take time, resources, and energy away from his own aims of success, and pour his life into his son? I never really asked why, and maybe that's because I never needed to. Dad has been telling me why since I was a boy.

Growing up, my dad constantly brought me with him in life. When he was going on a crazy adventure across the United States, he would bring me with him. When he was going out to our farm for a day of work, he would bring me with him. When he was going to clean the garage, he would force me to go with him. Whatever it was, my dad was constantly bringing me with him. It all had something to do with, as he's told me a thousand times, "raising me to be a leader."

My dad was the first one who taught me the greatest leadership lesson I've ever known, showing me by his own life and the way he raised me. But I wouldn't come to finally realize that lesson until now, after having it beaten into me by hundreds of other people.

Fundamentally, I guess you could define a leader as someone with followers. Simple. If you have followers, then you're a leader, and if you don't have followers, then you aren't a leader.

But here's a question: If all leadership means is a game to get followers, then what's the point? Yeah, maybe people will follow you for a bit, but someday, when you're body returns to dust, you won't be able to lead anymore—which means that in the end, you'll accomplish nothing more than leaving behind a bunch of lost people when you die.

Leadership is meaningless. Or I guess it would be if it were nothing but a game of followers. But that's not all it is. No, merely having followers is hardly a glimpse of what it means to be a leader.

It was October of 2015 when, during my visit to Atlanta, Georgia, Doug Carter of John Maxwell's leadership branch EQUIP Leadership told me during our interview, "Leaders are at their best not when they're focused on followers, but when they're focused on making other leaders."

And so goes the greatest leadership lesson I've ever learned: the highest calling of leaders is not to collect followers, but to forge leaders.

I've grown up listening to my pastor, Craig Groeschel, and many others I look up to always talk about the importance of "empowering others," and I remember once asking Mr. Groeschel what he meant by that. Also, I asked him why he does it at all when it would honestly seem far easier and more secure just to keep all the power of leadership to himself. But he didn't see it that way.

He answered me, "Because if we as leaders don't empower others, we become the lid to the potential of all we're doing. Holden, to be honest, I don't see it as safer or less risky to not empower people, because at the end of the day, I'm not betting on systems, strategies, products, or even myself or Life Church. None of that will last forever. I'm betting on the power of the gospel and on God's people."

Here's the truth: you won't live forever, so if you bet on yourself, nothing you ever do will matter forever. You will die, and if all you've ever done is collect followers, the fire inside you will die with you. To be a leader who starts something that matters forever, you have to place your bet on something that will last forever.

Chuck Black, the author of the *Kingdom Series* and *Knights of Arrethtrae*, told me during our interview, "God is not in the business of making puppets, but making leaders." At the time of hearing it, I'd thought it was just a cool generic comment about being a leader, but I've come to realize since then that it's so much more.

Jesus didn't come to earth and build an empire. He came to earth and built people. He didn't come and carve scripture into an indestructible stone; he came and carved it into the hearts of mankind. He didn't come and make people follow him, but rather, called people to follow him—which in the process, made leaders of his followers. As I've said before, I've learned that everyone follows something; the difference between followers and leaders is that followers are dragged by what they follow, and leaders pull others toward what they follow.

I don't presume to know why Jesus did things the way he did, but I can certainly learn from him. The fire he started 2,000 years ago burns a billion times brighter today, and that's not because he managed to become famous enough that the world could never forget him. No, what Jesus started then matters today because it was a fire lit in the hearts of people—leaders, warriors, and pioneers who would bring the fire to all nations.

Followers can catch fire to an extent, but they don't spread it. That's what leaders do.

Just as my heavenly father started an eternal fire by raising up leaders, so my earthly father is doing that with me and my siblings. Why does Dad pour his life into me, propel me, and raise me to lead?

Because every fire eventually dies, except one: the fire God lit inside you that you bring to others.

The fire in my dad can spread to me, and I can spread it to the world and pass it on to my children, and my children can spread it even further than I did and pass it on to their children. And their children can pass it on and on forevermore—for generations.

You're the gambler. You're betting the significance of your life on something, whether that be your mind, the potential of your success, how many people know your name when you die, the impact you have on the planet, or the impact you have on your children. You're the gambler—don't waste your bet.

Truly Live

There you have it. I started off this journey feeling like I was going insane, and in the end, a lot of people will probably think I did. After all, the line between insanity and faith is often blurred until you find faith yourself.

So take everything in this book as you please, because it's simply a compilation of what I've learned in life from others and what I've come to believe based on my own experiences. If you didn't like this book, that's okay. I'm young and inexperienced, and this is the first book I've ever written, so it's definitely got room for improvement. But I stayed true to myself throughout it—and in the end, being able to know I gave this book everything I had is more important to me than the response I get from it.

However, if this book did impact you or inspire you, let me make it clear that it wasn't me—it was my God, who lives in my heart and breathes through me.

With that, I have one last thing to say.

Catching fire with the spark of life and the wonder, passion, and adventure that come with it is part of what it means to truly live. But that's just the first step, and regretfully, it's also where most of us stop.

Why do we feel like we're suffocating inside? Maybe it's because we're afraid that if we let the fire of our heart engulf us and breathe the open air, we'll never again be able to contain it.

But that's the point. The spark of hope and life that Jesus brought to this world was never meant to be contained.

You want true life? Then stop clinging to the stuff you think you want, and lose yourself to what you can't live without. Time to give everything we have and everything we are to follow Jesus and carry hope to every last corner of the earth. After all, it's like he said: "Whoever would save their life will lose it, but whoever loses their life for my sake will find it" (Matthew 16:25).

To truly live, take the spark of life that burns inside you and bring it to others. You are here to radiate light and warmth to people just as if the sun burned inside of you—because the truth is, if you know Jesus, then something much brighter and hotter does burn inside you.

So come on, what are we waiting for?

Jesus brought the spark. It's time we bring the fire.

TAKEAWAYS

"Blessed is the one who finds wisdom, and the one who gets understanding, for the gain from her is better than gain from silver and her profit better than gold. She is more precious than jewels, and nothing you desire can compare with her."

—Proverbs 3:13-15

Because of the sheer amount of people and quotes included in my project, I was only able to include so much content in the prior chapters of this book. However, neither the quotes nor interviewees included in the earlier parts of this book should be assumed as more significant or meaningful, especially to me personally, than those which were not included.

Just so there is no confusion, let me make something clear: in my search for truth, God placed some people in my life at spectacular, cumulative moments, while placing others in the daily grind of building up to those spectacular moments. But without those who were part of the buildup, there never would have been anything spectacular.

Though it's small and petty in comparison, this final chapter is dedicated to all the incredible men and women who were part of my journey, and the ocean of wisdom they shared with me. Here, I have done my best to compile at least a few takeaways that have been most impactful to me personally which were not included in the earlier chapters. I hope these speak to you as much as they have to me!

Wisdom

"You can only see so far. In order to see more, you have to move farther in." —Joe Williams, head of NCF in Oklahoma, interview #2

"Quit trying to get people to heaven, and start bringing heaven to people." —Boe Parish, pastor, connector, founder and CEO of Corporate Care, interview #3

"No matter how bright and glamorous the world makes their agenda, our children will always see the brightest light as the one closest to them." —Greg Gunn, founder of Family ID, interview #12

"If you're being fake, no matter how good you are at it, people will always eventually see through whatever image you're holding up." —Rick Jones, Works24 sales representative, interview #14

"To live like others don't, you have to do what others won't." —Christopher Choate, Works24 sales representative, interview #16

"A fool doesn't learn at all, while a smart man learns from his mistakes, but a wise man learns from others who have gone before him." —Andrew Seldenrust, entrepreneur, interview #17

"You can't lead unless you're willing to follow, and you can't follow unless you're willing to lead." —Keith Wilmot, business CEO, interview #30

"Somehow, Satan has convinced so many of us we suck as warriors of God. That our prayers, words, and actions mean nothing. And here's what I've found: if you don't constantly remind yourself that those beliefs are a lie, you'll eventually come to believe they're true." —Mike Denison, business owner, entrepreneur, interview #32

"God did not say go into the church and make disciples, he said go into the world." —Harouff, youth outreach, YoungLife director of South Dakota, interview #35

"Speed of the leader, speed of the team." —Terry Payne, pastor, interview #36

"Success doesn't change people, it just magnifies who they already are." —Justin Mecklenburg, business owner, interview #38

"Sometimes you have to have tough love, because any small man can fire someone. But it takes a big man to bring the best out of people." —Chris McGahan, glass sculptor, business owner, interview #39

"Love must lead." —Melinda Brewer, financial advisor, interview #41

"An object that's moving is a whole lot easier to direct than one that's sitting still. So if you're wondering how to get started with something, do just that: start. Move. Seize whatever opportunity you have rather than wait for the perfect one. And as you start to move, God will direct you." —Dick Greenly, entrepreneur, founder of Water4, interview #45

"People want to follow the leader who fights on the front line." —Todd Brown, business owner, interview #46

"You can choose easy hard or hard easy." —Brian Robinson, VP of sales and marketing at Works24, interview #49

"One of Satan's greatest lies is safety. If he can get us to live for safety, then he can trap us there and prevent us from chasing our purpose." —Ray Sanders, president of The Cedar Gate, interview #50

"The relationships you don't give up on will become the best." —Georgia Cummings, mother and grandmother, interview #51

"If you never face and push through difficulty, you will never escape it." —Philip Edwards, Works24 sales representative, interview #52

"Self-confidence is very important, but self-reliance is very dangerous." —Ethan King, psychology student, interview #53

"Confidence that's based on what you do is never stable. Confidence must be based on who you are." —Sheri Yates, author, iKan Ministries, women's ministry, interview #54

"Our character is who we really are, our reputation is who people think we are. If we work on our character first, then our reputation will follow suit." —Larry Hughes, business owner, entrepreneur, interview #55

"God is going to show you the way to go and guide you through. All you have to do is be willing to follow." —Cary Gniffke, Works24 sales representative, interview #62

"Little steps take you much farther than you think they will, no matter whether the direction is good or bad." —John Seldenrust, oil and gas engineer, interview #63

"Until you're willing to do what God has called you to do, life will be empty." —Mark Susud, director of operations at The Cedar Gate, interview #65

"The biggest failure most of us experience isn't failing, but quitting." —Bill High, CEO of NCF Heartland, interview #67

"Seek to understand before being understood." —Emoly Walters, Miss Oklahoma Pageant winner 2010, interview #69

"In our day and age, despite our best intentions, protecting our children to the extent so many of us do is destroying them. If all we do is hide and shelter our kids from risk, they'll never learn what it takes to lead where it's hard and dangerous." —Tom Hill, entrepreneur, interview #71

"The most important part of scripture is living it." —Dave Jewitt, author, founder of Your One Degree, interview #73

"If you just want success, you can simply start some kind of project that benefits you. But if you want to truly change things and make a difference, you have to start a conversation—a movement—that reaches far beyond just you." —Scott Martin, founder of Odyssey Leadership Academy, interview #75

"I am where I am today because of God's favor, and because all the seeds I planted long ago I am now reaping the harvest of. Here's my advice to young people like you: I know you're young, but start planting seeds now. Don't wait." —Cliff Stockton, business owner, interview #76

"It's through taking risks that we learn about and discover more of ourselves." —Jon Cook, corporate chaplain, interview #79

"When seeking God's guidance, don't think so single-minded that, in waiting for him to speak directly to you, you neglect what he may say to you through someone else." —Danny Lane, businessman, interview #80

"You're not as important as you think you are, but at the same time, you're more important than you think you are. The man who can stand between those two extremes and hold the authority God has given him with an open palm and not command, but lead, is the one worth following." —Sam Roberts, pastor, head of campus operations at Life. Church, interview #81

"God can plant one seed, and reap an entire harvest. So never let yourself believe that you don't matter or that God can't use you." —Brian Banks, entrepreneur, interview #82

"Any feeling you have of control is an illusion. But trust God, and having control no longer really matters." —Frank Wheeler, inventor, entrepreneur, interview #83

"Most people hit failure and think they're going the wrong direction, when in reality, you have to go through failure to achieve success." —Eric Dubbell, senior VP of Primerica, interview #85

"Lose your life to save it. Seek to lose yourself to something greater than you." —Clay Steves, entrepreneur, interview #86

"Vision is occasionally shared in glamorous, amazing ways, but the most important and impactful way to share vision is through ordinary, daily interactions." —Bob Sullivan, business owner, interview #87

"We judge others based on their actions, but often judge ourselves by our intent. Learn to understand what you did, not what you meant to do." —Scott Beck, high school principal, interview #88

"One of the most important characteristics of a great leader is to develop leaders around them." —Jared Bowie, youth pastor, interview #89

"You can't be King David without being Shepard David." —Jerry Hurley, team development leader with Life.Church, interview #90

"If God led you there, he'll lead you through. You just have to hang on." —Kevin McCarty, attorney, interview #93

"All of our purposes have already been defined: love God with all your heart, mind, soul, and strength, and love your neighbor as yourself. People see God by how we love them." —Trevor Williams, pastor at Life.Church, interview #94

"Like settlers, too often people accept what is and conform themselves to it, failing to look to the horizon and ask the question not what is, but what can be?" —Lance Humphreys, entrepreneur, interview #96

"You deepen your message, God will widen your ministry." —Steve Green, chairman of the board of Museum of the Bible, president of Hobby Lobby, interview #98

"When you follow where God is calling you, some people will look at you and say that's crazy, that's dangerous, that's a risk. But in the end, it's the ones who have the faith to step out that are the ones God blesses." —Carry Summers, president of Museum of the Bible, interview #100

"People won't remember what you say or what you do, but they will remember how you make them feel." —John Davis, central group leader with Life.Church, interview #102

"People watch what we do more than what we say." —Austin Koehn, recruiter and business developer, interview #104

"Vision enables people with the power to give up what they are in order to become all that they can be." —John Gillespie, business owner, interview #105

"Nothing that happens to us is just for us." —Chris Beall, pastor at Life.Church, interview #106

"Don't overcommit, so in the end you don't underperform." —Chris Kuti, worship pastor, interview #107

"Life isn't so much about what happens to you, but what you do with what happens to you." —Jared Weston, marketing and business developer, interview #108

"Often, love is simple. It's just being there for people." —Rachel Gosz, aspiring nurse, interview #114

"Programs don't make disciples, people do. Disciples are handcrafted, not mass produced." —Bob Chambers, founder of PeopleLinQ, interview #116

"God sees us as precious. He doesn't see the scars on my arm, he sees his child." —Nathan Wilson, aspiring lawyer, interview #117

"If I choose not to forgive, it's like me drinking poison and waiting for the other person to get sick." —Dr. Herman Reece, OKC metro director of CBMC, interview #122

"What you do isn't what influences people. What really influences people is who you are." —Scott Klososky, international speaker and author, founder of FPOV, interview #123

"At times, a leader must be willing to walk alone." —Doug Eaton, business coach, interview #124

"Followers get told what needs done, leaders look for what needs done." —Randy Kamp, CEO of KampCo Foods, interview #126

"Be you in uncomfortable situations, because it's in those situations that you'll either learn to hide further behind a mask, or grow into more of the person you were born to be." —Scott Pruitt, former Oklahoma Attorney General, current United States administrator of Environmental Protection, interview #127

"Always remember where you're going, and always remember to enjoy the journey there." —Matt Palmer, director of marketing at Kimray, interview #128

"Focus on who you want to be, not who you don't want to be, because your car tends to veer toward what you're looking at." —Carmel Litz, mother, interview #130

"True friendships are made through real life experiences together." —Tracy Yates, business owner, interview #131

"How can you soar with eagles if all you ever do is run with turkeys?" —Nathan White, former United States Ranger, entrepreneur, interview #134

"Most people don't find their passion—their calling—because it's beyond expectation." —Scott Duncan, wealth advisor, interview #135

"Having faith doesn't mean you move without fear, but that you move in the face of it." —Dr. Richard Kopke, CEO of Hough Ear Institute, interview #136

"To build relationships, listen. Listening is not being quiet, but caring." —Ralph Mason, largest Sonic Drive-In franchisee, interview #141

"God doesn't remove doubt. If he did, you wouldn't have to trust Him." —Kent Bresee, entrepreneur, interview #142

"When you connect through success, you develop envy and competition. It's through vulnerability that people become true friends." —Tom Mboya, Kenyan medical doctor, motivational speaker, cultural leader, interview #143

Takeaways

"Christians without passion are spiritually asleep. They accepted God as their Savior, but not their Lord." —Harold Armstrong, area director of CBMC, interview #147

"Most people give up because they never had any real passion in the first place." —Randy Allsbury, founder of Allsbury Marketing, interview #148

"People never retire from a calling." —Leo Presley, leadership training and coaching consultant, interview #149

"When thinking about impact, don't skip your own backyard." —Wes Lane, former Oklahoma District Attorney, founder of Salt and Light Leadership Training (SALLT), interview #150

"People say go make a living. But no, I say go make a life." —Kirk Humphreys, former mayor of Oklahoma City, real estate entrepreneur, interview #152

"Being successful doesn't mean doing everything well, it means doing the right things well." —John Bingaman, businessman, interview #155

"Trust is earned by the drop, and lost by the bucket." —Mart Green, founder of Mardel Christian Bookstores, film producer, interview #156

"Don't focus on what you can get from people, but on what you can give." —Brent LaVigne, business professor at SNU, interview #157

"Hangout with leaders. Stay away from people who want power, and stick around people who have vision." —Travis McCoy, business owner, interview #159

"To press on even when it's hard, you have to have a purpose that's bigger than you." —Kayla Thompson, photographer, interview #160

"If fate throws a knife at you, there are two ways of catching it: by the blade, or by the handle." —Steve Saak, entrepreneur, interview #162

"Never let the money you can get from one place outweigh the love you have for something else." —Cameron Trice, co-president and CEO of JASCO, interview #164

"Real leadership is not when people obey you because they have to, but because they choose to follow you." —Jason Trice, co-president and CEO of JASCO, interview #165

"God's purpose for your life isn't accomplished at a destination, but on the journey." —Martin Hepp, civil engineer, business owner, interview #167

"Before God can work through you, he has to work in you." —Michael Jones, entrepreneur, founder of THRIVE Farmers coffee, interview #168

"No one really knows why they are alive until they know what they would die for." —Matt Hangen, missionary, COO of Water4, interview #170

"There are three levels of commitment: I'll try, I'll do my best, and I'll do whatever it takes. Try? You'll fail. Do your best? You'll do decent. Do whatever it takes? You'll succeed." —John O'Dell, Oklahoma director of FCA, interview #171

"You find success by exploring, not by waiting for it to find you." —Cheyn Onarecker, medical doctor, interview #172

"It's not what you do that really matters, but how and why you do it." —Chris Brewster, superintendent of Santa Fe South High School, interview #181

"How you leave one place is how you enter the next. How you leave one relationship, one job, one situation, whatever it is, is how you will enter the next." —Curtis Kupfersmith, entrepreneur, interview #183

"Don't waste your life. Every day, I learn how fleeting and how fast life will pass you by. You can't waste your youth, because what you do now will set you on a course for the rest of your life." —Josh Cockroft, Oklahoma state representative, interview #184

"Most people are desperate to live longer. For me, I want to live better." —Tony Tyler, VP of Tyler Media, interview #185

"Giving what you have may not change the world, but it will always change you." —Alan Barnhart, owner of Barnhart Crane, a $250 million dollar company of which he gives all profits away, interview #186

"When we're young, we want to live in tomorrow. But looking back now, I wish I had taken full advantage of and enjoyed the now rather than always trying to make it to the future where I imagined life would be bigger and better. Because the truth is, greatness isn't always loud." —Lee Truax, former president and CEO of CBMC, interview #187

"Children are given everything they want to keep them from getting what they need." —Janis Boydston, mother and grandmother, interview #188

"Try doing things for others just because you can. Because you're part of something bigger than yourself. If you do, it will completely change the way you live." —Robert Greenlaw, executive assistant at Kimray, interview #190

"Hard is what makes something great. You've got to love the hardness." —Todd Lamb, Lieutenant General of Oklahoma, interview #191

"The more comfortable you make it for people, the easier it becomes for them to live in denial of the danger surrounding them—and in many cases, this is what the Devil has successfully done to Christianity." —Doug Reeves, business owner, interview #192

"There's nothing uglier than a good-looking, arrogant guy." —Roxanne Parks, inspirational speaker, interview #193

"Freely give what you have freely received." —Jeremie Kubicek, author, speaker, entrepreneur, interview #194

"Never talk first. Listen to what everyone else is saying, pay attention and understand, and then talk last." —Joe Burnett, entrepreneur, interview #195

"Often, I try to help people, but fail to first look at where they are. To help people, you have to start where they are, not where you are." —Andrew Ranson, speaker, leadership developer, interview #196

"As a culture, we often don't train leaders. Rather, we train people to be equal. That's hogwash. We say 'He's shy, don't make him go talk in front of people.' No, it's just the other way around. He's shy, so go make him do it. We work at people's comfort levels instead of toward their abilities. We need to work toward and demand people's abilities, because to make leaders, we have to make people uncomfortable." —Calvin Burgess, business tycoon, missionary, interview #198

"Often, we look for things that work, but what if more than looking for things that worked, we aimed for things that last?" —Bob Goff, author of Love Does, speaker, interview #200

"Relax, and let the game come you to you." —Stephan Moore, former basketball player, leader of Camp Shiloh, speaker, interview #201

"Too often we try to prepare the road for our kids instead of our kids for the road." —Rick Krejci, business owner, interview #206

"The more you give, the more you live." —Tom Pace, entrepreneur, interview #209

"If you aren't sure about something, put it to the test. Sometimes, you just have to go and do it, whatever 'it' is, even though you might fail." —Matt Hankinson, youth outreach, area director of Youth For Christ, interview #211

"It doesn't take intentionality to be stretched, but it does take intentionality to grow from being stretched." —John Childers, outdoorsmen, program director with TeenPact Leadership Schools, interview #213

"Always remember that other people matter to God just as much as you do." —Hunter Hall, worship leader, interview #215

"As the leader, remember that methods are negotiable, but the vision God has given you is not." —Nate Kirby, worship leader, interview #219

"Take every thought captive, even if it seems insignificant, because deception happens a little bit at a time." —Rita Seldenrust, mother, interview #222

"Create relationship with your family while you're young, because

if you don't start to build that bond early on, it's hard to build later."
—Gigi Burk, mother, interview #223

"Anytime you have liberty, you'll have prosperity. When the people are free to do what they ought to." —Ralph Bullard, former headmaster of Christian Heritage Academy, school ambassador, interview #224

"Look at life as an adventure. There's always something around the corner. The hard things are preparing you for something ahead. Don't ever let life become mundane. When you see life as an adventure, you see problems as a challenge and opportunity to learn and grow." —Stan Lingo, entrepreneur, architect, interview #225

"To make a difference, we feel as if we have to do an amazing grand thing when honestly it can often be a simple touch." —David Howell, business owner, brain tumor survivor, interview #226

"Don't give out of duty. Give with joy or don't give at all." —Matt Benjamin, entrepreneur, interview #227

"Understand you're unique and one of a kind. Discover what that uniqueness is, and bring it to the world." —Dr. Nathan Baxter, leadership coach, interview #228

"The number one thing that holds people back is not being all in." —Mark Button, inventor, interview #232

"There are two kinds of people who never accomplish anything: those who never do what they're expected to do, and those who only do what they're expected to do." —Chuck Hyde, leadership and executive coach, interview #235

"The army of God was not meant to fight alone, but together." —Phil Smith, businessman, author, interview #242

"I want to see young people not give up on their dream. It's hard, and you'll fall down, but stay committed and eventually, you'll succeed. Because the fact is, the further you get into something, the higher probability of success you have." —Scott Thomas, founder of the worlds largest online retailer of precious metals, APMEX, interview #244

"I've realized it's not so much about what God has called me to do as it is who he has called me to be. What you do changes. Who you are rarely does." —Chad Missildine, leadership developer at Life.Church, entrepreneur, interview #245

"What does it mean for you to be generous? The answer to that question is different for every person, and that's the beautiful thing about it." —Daryl Heald, founder of Generosity Path, speaker, interview #248

"This world is a weekend stay at a hotel. Do you decorate a hotel room that you'll be at for just a couple days? No. That is just as this world." —Jaime O'Rourke, inventor, entrepreneur, interview #249

"God's got a habit of taking what the Devil meant for evil and doing something incredible with it. Of turning lemons into lemonade." —Dave Ramsey, financial broadcaster, motivational speaker, entrepreneur, interview #250

"The joy of life is in the moment. I'm a future-looking guy, and there's nothing wrong with goals and dreams, but when you place your heart in them you'll miss the moment." —Eric Joiner, business owner, interview #252

"To know one man well is to know all men better." —Kevin Jordan, entrepreneur, interview #253

"When the individual does right, the world is right. Our world is our reflection." —Kevin Stitt, entrepreneur, interview #254

"As long as you aren't willing to do anything God calls you to, you may miss the best thing." —Cassidy Litz, dancer, college student, interview #257

"People waste their time longing for tomorrow when all they have is today." —Kyle McCarty, poet, college student, interview #261

"Be intentional about the people you hang out with because it's those people that will either pull you forward or hold you back." —Ryan Fraser, college student, intern with Rolls-Royce, former intern with TeenPact Leadership Schools, interview #265

"Seize every opportunity you have. Don't let life just happen." —Elijah Knapp, creative-director with Telescope, interview #266

"By working up the strength to take the first step, you will have the courage to follow through." —Hannah Riegg, former intern with TeenPact Leadership Schools, interview #268

"To get people motivated for real, neither penalties nor rewards will work. For sold out, all in passion, you have to get people to buy into the vision itself." —Ty Tyler, CEO of Tyler Media, interview #271

"Condemnation leads to isolation, conviction leads to relationship." —Geoff Todd (GT), camp director with Kanakuk Kamps, interview #275

"Actions will always match someone's beliefs though their words may not." —Brad Thomas, president of Silver Dollar City, interview #276

"I try to figure out real quick if someone wants to just be someone, or if they want to do something. Seeking to merely be a politician or business executive is for power, but seeking a position in order to make a difference is something I want to be apart of." —Jay Hein, formerly with the leadership team with President George W. Bush, president of Sagamore Institute, interview #278

"You find courage through experience. David didn't start off fighting giants." —Kelly Shackelford, nationally acclaimed attorney, founder of one of the largest legal firms in America, First Liberty, interview #279

"Have an appetite for humility. I'm not talking about doing humble acts, I'm talking about being a humble person. Everything cascades out of humility." —Stephan Tchividjian, founder of NCF in south Florida, eldest grandson of Billy Graham, interview #283

"Take responsibly in failure, give the glory to others in victory." —Jason Grant, director of global leadership development at the John Maxwell Company, interview #287

"Lead where you are strong, team where you are weak." —Chris Goede, VP of the John Maxwell Company, interview #289

"Approach any brother realizing you are as bad as he is, and you will be received greatly." —David Knight, business owner, interview #290

"The secret to success is determined by your daily agenda, not one giant decision." —David Hoyt, president of the John Maxwell Company, interview #292

"The rains are going to be stronger than ever before for your generation, and so your foundation needs to be stronger than ever before." —David Wills, president emeritus of NCF, interview #293

"Often, we think people need instruction when what they really need is inspiration." —Doug Carter, senior VP of EQUIP Leadership, interview #294

"The spark that you pick up when you're young will determine the fire that's lit later on." —Peb Jackson, connector, author, interview #295

"Get caught up in God, not your calling, and once you get caught up in God your calling will come." —Angle Olson, mother, interview #310

"To impact people, catch them off guard. Surprise them. Do something that is not expected, and catch them in a moment of vulnerability." —Kyle Dillingham, violinist, musical artist, interview #312

"Take the risk that's in front of you. You can do more than you think you can." —Mike Liddell, oil and gas entrepreneur, interview #319

"Be open to transformation. God will chisel you if you let him." —Don Millican, CFO of Kaiser-Francis Oil Company, interview #320

"When you think something but aren't sure, you might not move. But when one other person comes alongside you and says I think so too, your suspicion changes to confidence. You have no idea how strong your encouragement and presence can be to people." —Wayland Cubit, lieutenant with the Oklahoma City police, interview #325

"You inspire people by how you live." —Cameron Shurtz, interactive development project manager with Life.Church, interview #326

"Life's not about what you want to be, but who you want to be." —Elise Hall, Oklahoma State representative, youngest State Representative ever elected in Oklahoma, entrepreneur, interview #327

"Advice is not always wise." —Ruth Powell, mother and grandmother, interview #328

"Underdogs win because they do things the way no one expects them to." —Lorne Hall, entrepreneur, interview #334

"You build trust by keeping it." —Dr. Anthony Jordan, executive director of Baptist General Convention, interview #335

"I don't regret anything, because I know God uses everything." —James Matush, entrepreneur, founder of a youth outreach center in memory of losing his teenage son in a rock climbing accident, interview #339

"The strength to stand up and fight is in all of us, we just have to wake it up, and we wake it up by just doing something. By doing that which our character propels us to do." —Wadid Daoud, businessman, interview #341

"Humility is a choice. And when you choose it over a long period of time it becomes character." —Shay Robbins, camp director of K-1 with Kanakuk Kamps, interview #342

"The decisions we make today, good and bad, determine where we end up tomorrow. So be wise in all you do, and remember that just because something is permissible doesn't mean it's beneficial." —Marty Grubbs, senior pastor of Crossings Community Church, interview #343

"Life is a whole lot more fun when you live it in community with others." —Derek Watson, filmmaker, interview #345

"To instill ownership in people, you have to be willing to give away some of it." —Bill Blankenship, college football coach, interview #346

"Even before the most exhilarating moments of your life, learn to find and feel peace." —Vince Parker, pastor at Life.Church, interview #347

"No matter where I place two dots on a chart, if they are both moving toward the same point then they are getting closer together. It's by growing closer to Christ that we grow closer to one another." —Jon Echols, Oklahoma State representative, entrepreneur, interview #349

"Do you want to fix the problem now? Then look in the mirror." —Brent Swadley, founder of Swadley's BBQ, interview #351

"It takes hardly anything to just be average. It takes just a little more to be a superhero." —Ron Swadley, Brent Swadley's father, interview #353

"Most of us knew who were once, but forgot. What I hope we can all remember is that in the end, the question that really matters isn't what am I going to do or where am I going to go, but who am I going to be?" —Una Mulale, pediatric critical care specialist, interview #364

"Don't be afraid to ask insane and impossible things of the only one who can make them possible." —Jason Ogan, youth leader, interview #370

"Truth is truth no matter where you find it." —Joey Sager, financial advisor, plane and helicopter pilot, interview #373

"Peace is not the absence of hard situations or circumstances, but confidence that God is with me in the midst of them and will see me through." —Debbie LoCurto, Executive VP of FPU church division, interview #375

"Never waste the opportunity to learn from an experience, whether good or bad." —Tyler Crabtree, youth outreach, interview #377

"There's nothing more unattractive than an unappreciative person. Show appreciation." —Alex Himaya, founder and senior pastor of theChurch.at, interview #380

"Wonder comes from curiosity, and curiosity comes from humility." —Mallee McGee, former intern with TeenPact Leadership Schools, interview #382

"Always remember that your word is your bond. You have to own your word, or it will stop meaning anything." —Laine Diffee, owner of Diffee auto dealership, interview #383

"Why tiptoe through life just to arrive at death safely?" —Steve Ridgeway, speaker, youth outreach, interview #386

"Take advantage of the fact people are different than you and have different opinions, and be open-minded enough to learn from them." —Hans Zeiger, Washington State Senator, interview #387

"I don't want to be a senator. What I want is to change things; to do something that matters, and being a Senator is one way of doing that." —Bruce Dammier, former Washington State Senator, current county executive of Pierce County, Washington, interview #388

"You're either going into a storm, coming out of one, or in one." —Keith Jossell, executive coach, interview #389

"The secret to the Christian walk, like golf, is in the dirt. In the action. Because it's in the doing of the Word that we truly understand it." —Sam Fox, director of compensation and benefits at Express Personnel, interview #390

"If I were to stress one thing to the next generation, it would be how important it is to really be yourself. God made you to be you." —Amena Brown, author, spoken word poet, interview #392

"Faith isn't faith until it's tested." —Susan Fox, mother and grandmother, interview #393

"If I can share in someone else's pain, my own pain is a gift I can give them." —Kevin Johnson, Works24 sales representative, brain aneurysm survivor, interview #394

"We seem to wonder how some people find such amazing opportunities in life. The truth is, we all have opportunities, the ones who have amazing opportunities simply took the ones they had." —Sam Herrmann, writing coach at Liberty University, former program director with TeenPact Leadership Schools, interview #395

"Jump small things first; you don't have to start off hurtling canyons. Start small, and then go big, which will also bring big reward." —Peter Martin, CEO of TeenPact Leadership Schools, interview #397

"You fall into leadership, you don't strive for it. I don't trust leaders who strive just to be in charge." —Jim Daly, CEO and host of Focus on the Family, interview #398

"As followers of Christ, it's a terrible assumption to say the world should be like us. That doesn't work. What works is to live according to what is right and lead by example, not force." —Mark Rodgers, political influencer, principal of the Clapham group, interview #399

"The world paints this picture that you have to choose between Christianity and adventure. That's a lie. Following Christ is not just worth it when you die, it's worth it right now." —Joel Trainer, assistant camp director with Kanakuk Kamps, interview #404

"Focus on depth, let God handle the breadth." —David Benham, speaker, author, entrepreneur, interview #406

"Strength comes through strain." —Jason Benham, speaker, author, entrepreneur, interview #407

"You can always reflect on what you have learned in the past, but it's what you're learning in the present that really inspires growth." —Aaron Watson, writer for NumberFire, former VP of operations at TeenPact, interview #408

"Operate with heart, mind, strength, and soul. Operate with all of it." —Charlie Hall, nationally acclaimed songwriter and worship leader, interview #410

"I was once told by someone that if I wasn't successful at the next place I went to, it was just my personality. I don't believe that. On the contrary, I believe that leaning into your uniqueness is exactly what will make you more successful than anything else." —Tyler Reagin, CEO of Catalyst Conference, interview #411

"Don't give up. Don't listen to the nay sayers and trash talkers. The reason they tell you that you can't is that they can't." —TJ Tomlin, Mixed Martial Artist, professional fighter, business owner, trainer, interview #412

"Success isn't taught, it's caught." —Larry Ross, publicist, business owner, interview #413

"Commit yourself to true, authentic relationship. We can't do this alone. Live it, and share it." —Jefferson Bethke, author, speaker, YouTuber, interview #415

"God doesn't believe in retirement, but he does believe in rehirement.

Keep going, God's not finished with you." —Ron Blue, founder of Ronald Blue Co., co-founder of NCF, interview 428

"Conquering something starts with now. Win the battle you are in now, and one after the other, and you will eventually win the war." —Mike O'Neal, president emeritus of OCU, interview #429

"You learn more by asking the right questions than by being taught the right answers." —Phil Cooke, film producer, writer, interview #431

"When you abide by rules, people will always find a way to get around them. Instead, abide by relationship." —Bob Funk, founder of Express Personnel, interview #433

"People may like you because you talk slick, but they'll trust you because of what you do." —Dick Adams, businessman, interview #434

"You don't have to say a lot to mean a lot." —Reburta Hill, my grandmother, pioneer woman, interview #435

"When all else fails, persistence prevails." —Phillip Jones, Works24 sales representative, interview #439

"It's hard for people to ever appreciate where they are and what they have without knowing what it takes to get there." —Chris Hill, helicopter pilot and head of aviation safety with the United States Coast Guard, interview #444

"Our greatest growth happens in times of challenges. That is when we are tested and pushed. That's when we are pulled to God. That's when our faith is activated." —Cord Sachs, developer of leaders, founder of FireSeed, interview #451

"To do something and to grow, showing up is the first step. If you don't show up you can't process what to change, or how to become more involved. So just show up, and step in." —Chad Johnson, chief of staff with the John Maxwell Company, interview #452

"Building your identity in the Lord is your primary defense in spiritual warfare." —Dennis Peacocke, speaker, author, founder of GoStretegic, interview #453

"A friend will tell you what you want to hear, a true friend will get in your face and tell you what you need to hear. You have to have people who will hold you accountable." —Brett Key, lieutenant with the Oklahoma highway patrol, interview #454

"It's the friends with you that will either keep you lazy or give you the strength to do what's hard and push through." —Kirk Hinnrichs, United States Coast Guard admiral, interview #462

"What you win them with is what you win them to." —Nathan Knight, church planter in Washington, DC, interview #464

"God does not find your joys too strong, but too weak. Christ is not about you saying no to bad things, but saying yes to something better." —Joey Craft, pastor, church planter in Washington, DC, interview #465

"If the light shining on you is brighter than the light shining within you, it will destroy you." —Paul Mundey, pastor, interview #466

"If you can take away the degree and titles and the man is still there, he's one worth going for." —Virginia Ali, co-founder of Ben's Chili Bowl, interview #467

"Don't ever fail to try a door just because you think it might be closed." —Ralph Drollinger, former NBA basketball player, founder of Capitol Ministries, interview #468

"I'm often asked, 'If you had to do it all over again, what would you do different?' Now, twenty years have passed in this church, and my wife and I generally answer that question that we wouldn't change anything. We would make the same mistakes we made, and try to learn the same lessons from them." —Mark Batterson, lead pastor of National Community Church, bestselling author, interview #470

"Memorizing the Bible from front to back without wisdom and understanding of it is worthless. A Ph.D. in theology is worthless without wisdom." —Demmise Bekele, Washington, DC taxi driver called to uplift and be a light to everyone who climbs into his car, interview #473

"Courage is a choice. Start practicing it in small ways, and then practice it in bigger ways. Find a way to be courageous every day." —Rex Crain, motivational speaker, interview #477

"Just step out in faith, and when you do, God will blow on your fire." —Jennifer Freeman, actress, interview #478

"The present is the only thing you have, and you only get it once." —Tripp Crosby, YouTuber, comedian, interview #479

If you're young, get this concept out of your head: age. What matters isn't age, it's wisdom. The anointing of God is older than anyone on this planet. When you pursue your anointing, you experience wisdom beyond your years." —Jeff Osborne, pastor, interview #482

"Enjoy life. The simplicity and innocence. It's the entire journey that makes crossing the finish line worth it." —Arthur Aidala, lawyer, legal analyst on Fox News, interview #484

"Learn what it means to abide in God. I hardly know. It's a journey that we were born to figure out. Abiding in God is the adventure of life, and it's coupled with the same exploring that comes with every adventure." —Matt Beacham, pro surfer, photographer, interview #485

"Our job is not to judge people, but to love them." —Sadie Robertson, motivational speaker, actress, interview #486

"'Follow me' doesn't have a destination, it has a person." —James Lankford, United States senator, interview #487

"The greatest adventure of life I know is abiding in God every day. Trusting him. Seeking his presence. I know of no adventure that's greater." —Noah Hamilton, cinematographer, interview #489

"Do not try to bypass the process of becoming the man or woman that God is calling you to be. There's no instant and immediate way to do it. You've got to go into the wilderness and be crushed. You've got to be sure your gifts and talents don't take you to a place your character can't keep you. Because if the spotlight shining on you is greater than the light shining in you, it will destroy you." —Christine Caine, motivational and evangelical speaker, author, activist, interview #490

"Stick it out. It won't come as easy or as quick as you think, so stick it out." —Nick Caine, co-founder and CEO of A21, interview #491

"We've got Jesus, we cannot lose. As followers of him, we should be the biggest risk takers there are." —Korie Robertson, TV star of Duck Dynasty, interview #492

"Saying I love you when you get married is one thing, choosing to love every day is another. And that's the part that really matters." —Frank Deprato, Works24 sales representative, interview #493

"You want people to see your content and say wow. If they don't say wow, keep working. Like polishing brass, one swipe doesn't get. It takes lots of criticism, time, and work to it to gleam." —Stephan Kendrick, film producer, interview #495

"It's not our job to change the direction of a person's heart, only God can do that. Our responsibility is simply to be there for people, love them, and be ready for God to use us." —Danny Sullivan, former program director with TeenPact Leadership schools, interview #496

"Mastery. It's something we've started to lose as a society, but that's more critical now than ever before. Being mediocre or simply adequate at something or a lot of things doesn't cut it anymore. Strive for mastery at something specific." —John Erwin, film director, film producer, interview #497

"It's through the struggle that God often gives us our message." —Andy Erwin, film director, film producer, interview #499

"We live in a world where it's easy to delegate the responsibilities of raising children. We can delegate changing diapers, education, feeding, most everything. And often, that's a good thing. But never delegate so much that you attempt to let someone else love your children for you." —Marla Hill, my mother, interview #500

"When I was your age, somebody once handed me a Bible and told me, 'Sin will either keep you from this book, or this book will keep you from sin.' And so, if there's one thing I would tell your generation, it would be to read the Bible, learn from it, and engage with it! Because, in the end, a Bible that's falling to pieces is usually owned by a person who isn't." —Levi Lusko, pastor, author, interview #501

"What wisdom can I share with you? It's one of those things I end up telling my kids a lot. They're young adults now. My word of wisdom is to own the responsibility of living your life as fully as you can, and not to just settle. Don't be afraid to own it, and don't be afraid to let things change. Seize life with all you have, and give it everything you've got." —Dudley Delffs, professional writer and editor, particularly the editor of this book as well as a mentor of mine throughout the writing process, interview #502

"You can always place more knowledge in your mind and more love in your heart. Never stop filling them." —Robert Mitchell, 25 years a fireman, retired Major with the Oklahoma City Fire Department, interview #503

"Be bold, reflect your claim. If you claim to be a follower of Christ, be bold in that and let all you do reflect it. Because people will watch what you do more than they'll ever listen to what you say." —Brett Burk, ranch and farm pharmaceutical representative, interview 504

"Who you become and the people you meet as a result of completing this project will be far more valuable than anything you ever make off of it." —Brian Hill, my father

And the list goes on and on, but the
pages have to end—for now.

ACKNOWLEDGMENTS

I feel like one of the most blessed dudes alive. I'm surrounded by people who love me, believe in me, push me, challenge me, and are there for me no matter what. How does some teenager from Oklahoma interview 500 leaders? Not by himself, I can tell you that. Not even close.

To my mom and dad: Marla and Brian Hill. Thank you both for your unconditional love and support. The first place I ever saw Jesus was in both of you.

To my siblings: Thank you Sienna for your never-ending selfless love, both in words and action. Thank you Brayden for your brotherly love and adventurous spirit, and for always providing me someone to pick on. Thank you Brianna for your challenging and inspiring voice, belief in and support of me, and weird sense of humor. And thank you Heston for being my longest held best friend, always on the grind with me and always there for me even if I'm being a jerk. I'm humbled that I get to be the big brother of four world-changing warriors of God.

To my extended family: I'm beyond grateful to be surrounded by such a loving and encouraging, and at times, crazy family. The legacy I get to be part of carrying on is because of you all.

To the families of my Life Group and that I grew up alongside: Thank you for loving me as one of your own, the loads of fun we've had together, and for showing me what it means to live in community.

Acknowledgments

To the Works24 sales team: In so many ways, y'all were the reason I even started my crazy project in the first place. The drive, humility, and passion in each of you have always inspired me, and always will.

To all 500 interviewees: I wish I had room to list every one of you here. Thank you all for your investment in me, belief in me, and your heart to spend time with some random teenager who owed you nothing and who offered you nothing—but who will forever be different because of you and grateful to you.

To the team of people who helped make this book a physical reality: Thank you for your dope work, coaching, advice, inspiration, challenging ideas, and encouragement. And a very special thank you to my beast writing coach and editor, Dudley Delffs.

To the men and women who have mentored me: I know I can very easily become overbearing and stubborn, and I'm pretty sure that if were in y'alls shoes I would have told myself as much by now and been done with me. But for whatever reason, y'all have stuck with me, and have never stopped believing in me. For that and so much more, thank you.

To my Savior, King, and Father: Jesus Christ. This story is yours. Thank you for the chance to live it. I love you, Father.

NOTES

To know more about any of the individuals, events, camps, brands, businesses, ministries, or places mentioned in this book, please visit holdenhill.com for a list of corresponding information.

HOLDEN HILL

is an American born lover of Jesus Christ, adventurer, author, and aspiring motivational speaker. Holden is the son of two entrepreneurial parents and is the oldest of five siblings. Throughout high school, his unquenchable curiosity led him on a journey of seeking truth from 500 Christ-following leaders. Through that journey, God used Holden's personal struggles and battles to erupt an untamable fire in his heart for Jesus—a fire that he now sees as his calling to spread across the world.

For inquiries regarding Holden, such as speaking opportunities and interview requests, please visit www.holdenhill.com